Oh, Dear Life!! And how wonderful when we're able to win a bit or all of it back for a time.
—Lynn Kotula

i carry your heart with me(i carry it in my heart)
—e e cummings

CARRYING THE TIGER

CARRYING THE TIGER

Living with cancer, dying with grace,
finding joy while grieving

TONY STEWART

WEST END BOOKS
NEW YORK, NEW YORK

Author website: www.TonyStewartAuthor.com

Hardcover ISBN: 979-8-9922649-2-0
Paperback ISBN: 979-8-9922649-1-3
Ebook ISBN: 979-8-9922649-0-6
Audiobook ISBN: 979-8-9922649-3-7
Library of Congress Control Number: 2024927637

Publisher's Cataloging-in-Publication
(Provided by Cassidy Cataloguing Services, Inc.)
Names: Stewart, Tony, 1955- author.
Title: Carrying the tiger : living with cancer, dying with grace, finding joy while
          grieving / Tony Stewart.
Description: New York, New York : West End Books, [2025]
Identifiers: ISBN: 979-8-9922649-2-0 (hardcover) | 979-8-9922649-1-3
          (paperback) | 979-8-9922649-0-6 (ebook) | 979-8-9922649-3-7
          (audiobook) | LCCN: 2024927637
Subjects: LCSH: Stewart, Tony, 1955- | Married persons--Biography. | Cancer--
          Patients--Family relationships. | Grief. | Wives--Death--Psychological
          aspects. | Loss (Psychology) | LCGFT: Autobiographies. | BISAC: FAMILY &
          RELATIONSHIPS / Death, Grief, Bereavement. | SELF-HELP / Death, Grief,
          Bereavement. | BIOGRAPHY & AUTOBIOGRAPHY / Memoirs.
Classification: LCC: RC265.6.S74 A3 2025 | DDC: 362.1969940092--dc23

Note from the author: This is a work of nonfiction. Events and conversations are as I remember them. Some names were changed to protect privacy and some events were compressed. Any mistakes are my own.

Contents

Author's Note

In Dante's *Inferno*, the gates of Hell bear the inscription: "Abandon all hope, ye who enter here." This is not that story.

This is a book about how my wife, Lynn, and I navigated severe illness and its aftermath without abandoning hope. Together we found caring doctors, weathered life-threatening setbacks, learned to live fully in the shadow of death, and shared the intimate grace of her departure from this world. Then, with the help of old friends and new, I climbed out of shattering grief and eased my way towards new love. There was uncertainty, fear, and sorrow, yes, but also tenderness and joy, and I had the honor and privilege of accompanying Lynn on her final journey.

I wish I had been able to read something like this when we embarked on our odyssey, stunned, scared, and unsure of what lay ahead. I hope it will help others find their way forward or make peace with what they've already experienced. Although your circumstances may be different from mine, the underlying story is universal and all too rarely shared.

Tony Stewart
September 2024

PROLOGUE

Wednesday, February 10, 2021
www.CaringBridge.org/LynnKotula

Lynn is leaving us faster than I expected.

Once we made the decision to stop treatment, she quickly turned in on herself, lost in thought much of the time. We had a good conversation last night, but more often her attempts to communicate are just fragments, not all of them coherent. She hardly eats, and I am no longer trying so hard to encourage her. She says she's not ready to go yet, but her actions suggest otherwise.

The hardest part is coming to terms with the fact that my love is no longer enough to keep her with us.

I don't expect Lynn to look at her email again or read texts, but I have been reading them to her, along with your comments posted here. If you would like to visit or speak with her, I encourage you to do so sooner rather than later. During daylight is probably best; she drifts off somewhere after dark and then sleeps soundly for many hours.

Unfortunately, getting out of bed in the morning, which she wants to do, is now unbelievably painful because of her neck. I don't know how many more days she will be willing to endure the pain. But I treasure our nights together when it is just the two of us. Even in silence we feel each other's presence.

Right now, we are sitting together in the kitchen, where she can look out at the river. I read her the first half of this post already, she smiled and nodded. I will read the rest to her now.

27 comments

Tony, I am so, so sorry. I love Lynn, too, and would just wish her a life without pain. —Jane

Would that love were enough. It is not. But, in the end, it's all we really have. Fill the time you have with it. —Dave

PART ONE

LIVING
WITH CANCER

"It's not the cancer that's killing me, it's the diarrhea."

Bad News

Sunday, September 28, 2014

It's an unseasonably warm Sunday in late September. I am working at my computer while my wife, Lynn, lies on our bed across the hall, sketching our elderly cat, Jack.

She's spent a lot of time like that these past two months, feeling increasingly crummy for some reason the doctors can't figure out. It began as chronic indigestion, then acid reflux, and recently bouts of diarrhea. She's stopped enjoying her meals and is losing a lot of weight.

Her doctors have given her every kind of scope and scan they can think of— endoscopy, colonoscopy, and gastrointestinal CT—but her internal plumbing looks fine. She also had a spinal MRI last week because of a knot of pain in the middle of her back, but none of them expects much from that. They figure it is "referred pain," experienced there but originating elsewhere.

When Lynn's phone rings, I don't think much of it, but as she speaks her voice tightens. She says, "Hi, Dr. Weinstein," then, "Yes, I understand," and finally, "What should I do?"

When Lynn hangs up, I walk into the bedroom, where she looks up with a puzzled expression. "That was Dr. Weinstein," she says, "calling about the MRI. He says there's something in my spine that shouldn't be there, and behind it they can see something in my lung that shouldn't be there. They can't say for sure, maybe it's myeloma or some kind of lymphoma, but more likely tumors. I need to see an oncologist right away."

I am stunned. Lynn is a vibrant, youthful sixty-eight-year-old who moves through the world with a smile on her face. She doesn't smoke, walks everywhere, easily climbs the five flights of stairs to her studio, and swims sixty lengths in the Columbia University pool five times a week. Just six months ago, she quit her part-time job so she could devote herself to painting full time. How can this be?

Lynn calls her sister but doesn't want to talk to anyone else, so she asks me to email several of our closest friends and let them know the news. It doesn't occur to us to keep it a secret.

Then I go to the pool to swim out my fear and frustration – why did these symptoms take so long to figure out? – while Lynn spends the afternoon on our bed, letting the news sink in.

✍

Lynn and I met in 1985 at the Columbia University swimming pool in New York City. She was an artist, thirty-nine years old, who supported herself by waiting tables. She had not been in a relationship for some years and had reconciled herself to the likelihood that she would be single for the rest of her life.

Lynn and Tony in 1993

I was twenty-nine, a filmmaker, ten years younger, and in the process of getting divorced. I was on the rebound, noticing all the women around me as I tried to reassure myself that my life was not over.

One day Lynn crossed from one lane to another in front of me and I said something like, "Why were you swimming in that lane? You usually swim in a faster one." I think those were the first words I ever spoke to her.

"I was kicking" she replied, so she chose a slower lane.

I thought nothing of it. The next day, when she was doing leg stretches at the end of my lane and I talked to her again, I assumed it was a coincidence.

Later Lynn told me that she was so surprised by this guy paying attention to her, aware of which lane she swam in, that she decided I must be wildly attracted to her. She deliberately stopped and did leg stretches so we would have an opportunity to talk. What she didn't know was that I was talking to everyone—or at least, to all the cute women—and hadn't noticed her in particular. This misunderstanding led to our thirty-five-year relationship.

I fell for Lynn during our second or third conversation at the end of the lane in the swimming pool, when we admitted that we would like to see each other on dry land. I said, "I'm free every night this week except Wednesday, when I have to stay home because I volunteer for the Rape Crisis Intervention Program at St. Luke's Hospital." And without missing a beat, she said, "Oh, so you stay home on Wednesday nights and nobody gets raped?"

So quick, so clever, so confident. I mean, who would say such a thing to a near stranger, a joke implying that I must be a rapist, so my staying home would protect women. And how did she know I would find it funny?

Three days later, I attended the opening of Lynn's first solo painting exhibition. Afterwards, we went out to dinner with a dozen of her friends, then shared a taxi uptown where we sat up until 2 a.m. in a late-night dive, drinking beers and talking, while she kicked off her shoes and put her feet up on my side of the booth, touching my thigh. Then I walked her to her building, and we agreed that we would like to see each other again.

But just before that, after this amazing long evening, standing on the sidewalk in front of her stoop, I said, "I'd really like to see you again, but I saw your resume at the opening, and I'm afraid you're a lot older than me."

"That's okay, we're only going on a date," she said. "It's not like we're getting married."

When Lynn and I got married, three years later, she was forty-two, and we were trying to have a baby. We had lived together for two years but were a strikingly unromantic couple, and neither of us had ever suggested marriage. Then, one day, Lynn said, "You know, Tony, getting married would be a much smaller thing than having a child, because you can always undo a marriage, but you can't undo a child." And then she added that my medical insurance was better than hers, "so if I get pregnant, we will want me to be on your insurance, which will only work if I marry you beforehand."

That was how Lynn proposed to me.

We never did have children, but we were married the next week by a Justice of the Peace, with about eight friends and family members in attendance.

Throughout our marriage, Lynn insisted on just two things: I had to tell her what I was thinking, and every kiss had to be a real kiss: Your lips had to be alive. If I gave her a peck while trying to rush out the door, she would grab me and hold me back saying, "That wasn't a real kiss," and make me do it again and do it right.

From our earliest dinners together, she always wanted to know what I was thinking, and if I said, "Nothing much," she wouldn't accept it. "That's not possible," she would say. "You have to be thinking something. Tell me." And I would force myself to come up with something.

Over time, I started anticipating the question, and as I went through the day I would try to notice and remember my more interesting thoughts—a quirky-looking person that I passed on the street, an observation about the state of the world—and bring them back to her like presents.

Then she moved on to, "What are you feeling?" and I learned to do the same with my feelings.

Lynn loved kissing and talking, preferably at the same time. The talk didn't need to be sexy, it could be on any topic at all. We just had to have our heads close together, and in due course the soft shocks between our lips would work their magic. "Breathe," she would say, "breathe out for me." Then she would inhale and purr as if I'd given her the greatest gift in the world.

Lynn with her cat Merry Cherry

Most of all, Lynn was an artist.

She was known for her carefully composed still-life paintings: squashes and pears, pitchers and vases, eggplants and lemons arranged on a tabletop like a miniature stage set. Before starting a painting, she would spend hours or even days creating a striking tableau, followed by several weeks of intense focus as she brought the painting to life, brushstroke by brushstroke.

Her studio was in a hundred-year-old walkup apartment that she herself had renovated, spackling the walls and stripping paint from the window frames. Six large windows looked out over neighboring rooftops, flooding it with light. She slept in a tiny bedroom at the back and converted the living and dining rooms into an L-shaped studio, with racks of paintings and art supplies along the walls, and an easel in each room so she could work on two canvases at a time.

Making art and experiencing art filled Lynn with energy and joy; she was never more alive than when creating a painting or encountering one for the first time. She felt that art brought beauty and meaning to a chaotic world, and she lived to make more of it and share that joy with others.

"Pudding Mold and My New Box", 2006

Lynn had talent, friends, vivacity, and the gift of openness. I was more private, a cheerful introvert, except when I was running one of the big projects that filled my career. When I was making a movie, designing software, or speaking at a conference, I felt comfortable; I had purpose and was happy and engaged. But at home and in our social life, I let Lynn take the lead.

For a while, I had a job that required flying back and forth to Europe, earning thousands of frequent flyer miles. So we decided to use those miles to vacation somewhere far away, where we could be together in a world as unlike New York City as possible.

On our first trip to India, in 2002, we hired a car and driver to take us to Dungarpur, a small city where Lynn had heard about a fifteenth-century "painted palace" that sounded intriguing. The palace had never been modernized, there was no electricity or running water, but a caretaker walked us through it from top to bottom, opening the shuttered windows on each floor. From outside, it looked unremarkable: a plain white five-story tower. But inside, it was striking, with dozens of intricate Rajasthani frescoes covering every inch of the walls, gleaming in the bright squares of sunlight.

Afterwards, we wanted to walk, so we asked our driver to meet us at the bottom of the street that wound downhill to the city gates. As we neared the city center, the houses gave way to small shops. We paused at every window, admiring the unfamiliar items on display. Around us, locals stared with open curiosity; it was clearly uncommon to see western tourists here.

We were outside what we imagined was a hardware store when the shopkeeper, a young man, came out and asked, in halting English, where we were from. Excited to learn that we had come all the way from America, he said, "Please, follow me. I want you to meet my parents." Lynn and I exchanged a glance—was this safe?—but his warmth seemed genuine.

He led us across the street and into a small house where he introduced us to his somewhat startled parents, then left us alone with them because he had to get back to the shop. The parents were very polite but spoke almost no English. For twenty minutes, the four of us sat on the floor of their living room, sipping tea and communicating mostly with smiles and nods, while the father took what appeared to be family photos off the walls and explained them to us in words we didn't understand. Then, with handshakes all around, we excused ourselves and continued on our way, thrilled at having been invited into their lives.

Lynn and I returned to India seven more times. We stayed in small hotels off the beaten track, ate vast quantities of delicious food (using our fingers when cutlery wasn't offered), and walked freely through towns and villages where we rarely felt unsafe. Everywhere we went, strangers invited us into their homes and shared their lives with us. And everywhere we went, Lynn had wonderful interactions with the kids who played in the streets. She was energetic, funny, and warm, and they followed her like a pied piper.

For thirty-five years, I called Lynn "Cutie" and she called me "Pussycat" (or, occasionally, "Bob"), but we never celebrated Valentine's Day, rarely gave each other presents, and hardly ever said "I love you." Instead, Lynn told me that I was her best friend, and I told her the same.

Leading a game of Simon Says, India 2011

Sunday, September 28, 2014

When I return from the pool, we sit together in the kitchen, facing each other across the small table and holding hands. After all those years, when we assumed we would quietly grow old together, suddenly our time has an end point, and words that never felt comfortable come tumbling out.

We stroke each other's hands and say, "I love you" again and again, probably more than we have in our entire marriage. We say, "You're the best thing that ever happened to me." We remind each other of joyful experiences we shared, our travels in India and Asia, difficult times when we relied on each other for advice and support. We cry and smile and cry again. And we wonder how much time we have left, and what we can do to get more of it.

Monday, September 29, 2014

Dr. Weinstein is an old-school doctor of the kind that has almost disappeared: A sole practitioner in a wood-paneled office who draws the blood samples himself. When Lynn asks him what she should do, he recommends that we see a friend of his, Dr. Khalid Dar, an oncologist at the local hospital; they lunch together once a month.

We consider calling Memorial Sloan Kettering Cancer Center, one of the most prestigious cancer hospitals in the world, which happens to be right here in Manhattan. But we have both heard horror stories, not about the quality of care there but about the attitudes of the doctors. Several friends tell us cautionary tales about surgeons at Sloan Kettering who took a "my way or the highway" approach and oncologists with no bedside manners. We have known Dr. Weinstein for years, he feels more like a friend than a doctor; and Dr. Dar is affiliated with Mount Sinai, a very good hospital within walking distance. We decide to trust Dr. Weinstein and follow his recommendation.

First thing Monday morning, we call Dr. Dar's office and ask for an appointment. His secretary, Arlene, is sympathetic, but Dr. Dar doesn't have an opening until Wednesday.

Waiting until Wednesday feels like agony. We imagine the tumors growing rapidly, and that every minute we aren't dealing with them makes it more likely they will be unstoppable. I obsessively google the terms Dr. Weinstein used— "myeloma," "lymphoma," "metastasis"—hoping to find explanations that do not involve advanced cancer. There aren't many.

Lynn starts emailing her friends to tell them what's happening. She has a large circle of friends with whom she keeps in contact, and it feels like the most natural thing in the world to turn to them. We don't realize what a significant step this is.

She could have kept quiet, waited until she knew more, perhaps told only a few of our closest friends, and her course of treatment would probably have been different. In fact, it definitely would, since one of her first emails reaches a friend who suggests contacting a doctor she knows at Yale New Haven Hospital, which will open the door to an entirely different path.

Equally important, we are starting to form our own support group.

From: Lynn Kotula
Date: 9/29/2014
Subject: Nasty News

Dear Susannah,

Right now, I am waiting to talk to the doctor who ordered the MRI last week. My GP received the report and called to tell me the results—two masses in my right lung and something on my 10th and 11th vertebrae that the radiologist called a possible myeloma, lymphoma, or metastasis. Tony talked to the head of oncology at Yale who said that I will probably need a biopsy of the spine— first—and then of the lung, just his guess, in the next few days.

I have an appointment Wednesday with an oncologist, who will help me figure out in what order we should do the biopsies (spine or lung first?).

I keep imagining that they sent me the wrong results and that I'm just fine. We're pretty scared. I never in a million years thought that there was anything significant wrong with me and, of course, hope that that's still the case.

Thought I should let you know as you've listened to me complaining these past few weeks. I would talk to each of you but have to leave the phone lines open.

Lynn sent variations on this email again and again, and her friends replied with shock and dismay. Soon there were dozens of emails flying back and forth; managing and responding to them began sucking time and energy we couldn't spare.

Then someone suggested setting up a private web page on a site called CaringBridge, where we could post information in one place and our friends could respond at their convenience. Thus, the "Lynn Kotula" CaringBridge journal was born.

At Lynn's request, I wrote almost all the posts. Although she was willing to talk about her cancer in one-on-one conversations, writing about it, even in a closed forum, made her feel too exposed. But Lynn reviewed each post and often had me make small edits—mostly removing references to her fear and some of the nastier side effects. She wanted her friends to know about the cancer and be able to track her treatment, but she didn't want them to feel sorry for her or let the cancer define her. She wanted to have the exact same conversations she'd always had.

Friends told us they enjoyed reading the posts, watching over our shoulders as we learned to navigate the hospitals and doctors, the setbacks and side effects. "I'm in the middle of several books right now, but the serial narrative of Lynn's situation is by far the most interesting," wrote our friend Ann. "Thank you for allowing us to be in the room with you."

At the height of Lynn's treatment, almost 200 friends were reading each post, clicking the "like" button and writing comments. The majority were straightforward expressions of love and support—"So sorry to hear what you're going through!" and "I'm thinking of you every day." But even the most mundane ones gave us strength and a sense that we were part of a community. It was like having our own dedicated cheerleading squad, just when we needed one the most.

Eventually, the cancer defeated the drugs and Lynn died beside me. At this point, I assumed I would stop writing; after all, it was the "Lynn Kotula" journal. But I couldn't. The act of writing had become integral to my healing, and as I continued writing in the days after Lynn's death, exposing my emotions as I never had before, friends told me how much they learned about themselves from the twists and turns of my grief, and the somewhat surprising events that followed.

This book is a direct result of those comments. I've filled in gaps, edited the posts, and changed a few names, but this is the story as I lived it.

Into the Whirlwind

Wednesday October 1, 2014

Promptly at 10:00 a.m., we present ourselves at Dr. Dar's office in a slightly faded medical building across the street from our local hospital.

Dr. Dar appears to be from South Asia, either Indian or Pakistani, and his soft manner is immensely appealing. As soon as he sees us, he comes out from behind his desk and gives Lynn a big hug, which is surprising and satisfying. She has been shaking for three days; she needs this.

Dr. Dar tells us that Lynn's tumors fit a classic profile: They are almost undoubtedly lung cancer that has metastasized to her spine. Which means she has stage IV cancer.

"It happens all the time," he says. "The tumor grows in your lung, you don't feel anything, and then it spins off a metastasis that lands in your spine where you finally start to feel it. The biopsy may tell us it is something else, but that would be very surprising."

We start to ask about treatment, but Dr. Dar says that will depend on the tests he needs to order: A biopsy of the larger lung tumor, and a PET scan of Lynn's entire body to see whether there is active cancer anywhere else. But the lung cancer can't be treated right away; first, the tumor in Lynn's spine needs to be addressed.

"It's right on top of your spinal cord, and it's growing. We have to stop it before it paralyzes you."

In short, Lynn needs to see a neurosurgeon right away.

Somehow, this hadn't occurred to us. In ten minutes, we have moved from a gentle hug to the likelihood that Lynn has stage IV lung cancer to the need for an immediate consultation with a neurosurgeon. I feel like Alice tumbling down the rabbit hole, with no idea of where we'll land.

Dr. Dar knows a young neurosurgeon, Dr. Kevin Yao, who has impressed him at seminars. While still with Dr. Dar, we call Dr. Yao and are elated to discover that he can make an opening for Lynn this afternoon, just two hours from now. But he needs us to bring a CD of Lynn's MRI, so he can see the images for himself. This is a problem: We don't have a CD. We only have the written report.

Lynn calls Lenox Hill Radiology and they tell us we are in luck: We can get the CD if we go to their IT department in a townhouse on the upper east side. We skip lunch and grab a cab, taking it first to the townhouse, where we wait while they cut a CD for Lynn, and then up to Dr. Yao's office near Mt. Sinai Hospital, arriving just in time for the appointment. It all feels very rushed and scary, and I have to take the whole day off from work rather than the couple of hours I had planned.

Dr. Yao is in his thirties and movie-star handsome. He spends a lot of time with us, carefully reviewing the images of Lynn's spine and then turning the screen so we can see them. There are two dark-colored lumps close together in her spine; the larger of them is just a few millimeters from the white strand that is her spinal cord.

"This one is critical," he says. "Depending on how fast it grows, it could start pressing on the cord in a matter of days." Once that happens, Lynn will start to lose control of her legs. "The longer we let the pressure continue, the more likely it will be permanent."

But Dr. Yao isn't sure neurosurgery is the way to go. If he operates, it will be weeks before Lynn is strong enough to start chemo. He suggests that we try intensive radiation instead. "There's a new technology called IMRT—Intensity-Modulated Radiation Therapy. It can be done in a single session, and the recovery time is short."

We ask about the downsides and Dr. Yao assures us they are relatively minor. "In the long run, your spine may be damaged both by the tumors and by the radiation that will kill them. But that doesn't always happen, and if it does, there are procedures to repair the damage that don't require full surgery."

Dr. Yao tosses off their names, but I don't write them down. They seem too far away to worry about. We just need to get through the next few weeks and kill the tumors as quickly as possible. It is all scary, but Lynn feels she has no choice.

∽

"What should we tell Mom?" asks my sister, Francie, that night. It is not a trivial question.

Our mother, Shirley, is eighty-six years old and lives alone. She used to be fiercely independent, but she's lost her short-term memory and the ability to make decisions, and now she's losing her mobility, too. Caring for her is bringing Francie and me closer together than we have been in years.

But Shirley is still very good at two things: Worrying about her two adult children and telling us what to do.

A few years ago, when Francie was briefly hospitalized, she made the mistake of telling Shirley, who promptly flooded Francie and her husband with phone calls, asking for updates and offering unsolicited advice. She couldn't let go of her anxiety, couldn't accept that Francie, Paul, and their doctors might know what was best.

Now, Lynn and I face even worse challenges. The last thing we need is my mother calling every five minutes and staying up all night worrying about us. But we also don't need the anger that will follow when she finds out we kept something this important from her.

Francie and Shirley

"Maybe we don't tell her anything," I suggest. "At least not now. Until we know what we're doing."

"Sounds good," agrees Francie. "She has a hard time with uncertainty."

So I continue to have dinner with my mother every Tuesday on the way home from work, and Francie continues to call her almost every day, but we don't mention Lynn. When Shirley asks about her, we say something noncommittal and change the subject.

Friday, October 3, 2014

Dr. Dar sends Lynn for a full-body PET/CT scan, the first of many tubes she will lie in over the next few months. Unlike the detailed images in an MRI, Lynn's PET scan looks like a fuzzy infrared photograph of her entire body, with areas of abnormally high metabolic activity—an indicator of cancer—overlaid on her silhouette like bright red thunderstorms on a weather map.

Lynn's scan reveals two small thunderstorms in her lung and two in her spine, the same tumors that we already know about, and nothing more. Dr. Dar tells us this is good news: We have a chance to stop the cancer before it spreads further.

The neurosurgeons need a better view of Lynn's spine, so on Sunday she spends three hours in the basement of Mt. Sinai's main building having six more spinal MRIs while I wait on a bench across the street in Central Park. But I'm unable to relax, so from the bench I send an update to Dr. Steve Gore, my friend of a friend who is head of medical oncology at Yale New Haven Hospital. I'm not sure what I'm looking for, but Yale is a prestigious place. I want to keep our line of communication open.

Steve replies within a few hours: "Wow, Tony, that's a lot. Sounds like they're doing all the right things."

It feels like a lot to us, too. It's comforting to hear that even an expert finds Lynn's case complicated.

The next day Lynn and I are back in the Mt. Sinai basement, waiting to be inducted into the mysteries of radiation oncology. We sit side by side on plastic chairs in a small brightly lit office, the antechamber of a high-tech temple. Around the corner is the linear accelerator that will power Lynn's radiation, and down the hall are the MRI machines where she spent the previous afternoon.

First, a physician's assistant, then a nurse, and finally a resident come in to see us, full of smiles and reassuring warmth, each sitting across from us in the same chair, asking the same questions about Lynn's health history, symptoms, and diagnosis. By the time Dr. Cheryl Brown enters, we've grown tired of the repetition.

Dr. Brown is brisk efficiency, friendly but devoid of warmth, making me wonder if the cheerful resident who preceded her will lose her bubbly charm as she grows into her career.

Dr. Brown asks no questions; she tells us what to expect and answers ours. She confirms that the team thinks intensive radiation is the preferred treatment for Lynn's spinal tumors. "Radiation will kill them with less impact than traditional surgery," she says. "There's no wound to heal afterwards, and the recovery time will be comparatively quick."

Seven doctors were involved in this decision. "They don't know what you look like," says Dr. Brown, "but they'd recognize your MRI if they saw it in the street."

At the time, I am working as an administrator for a small organization that takes care of teenagers with mental illness. Besides the satisfaction of doing some good in the world, I am especially lucky because my hours are flexible, and I am able to do a lot of my work from home. When I tell my colleagues about Lynn's tumors, they are deeply sympathetic and encourage me to take care of Lynn first and worry about work second.

So, even during these first intensive weeks, I am able to be with Lynn at most of her appointments, taking notes that we later review to see if she remembers things the same way. Often she doesn't, and we spend hours reconciling our memories about important conversations. It is striking how differently we remember the details of each meeting: what was said, in what order, what seemed most important. Sometimes it feels like we are basing important decisions on shifting sand.

Next up is the biopsy of Lynn's lung tumor, a prerequisite for everything that will follow. It doesn't matter that everyone agrees this is lung cancer; Medicare and the hospital both require a formal diagnosis. Doctors will insert a needle through Lynn's back while she lies in a CT scanner and, guided by live images, extract a small amount of tissue from one of her tumors. From this bundle of cells, the pathologists will determine what type of lung cancer Lynn has, and part of it will be sent out for a more detailed genetic analysis.

"The lung cancer diagnosis takes just a few days," says Dr. Dar. "As soon as we have that, the radiation can proceed. The genetic analysis can take a week or more and will determine the best type of treatment for your cancer."

The default is chemotherapy, but if Lynn is lucky her tumors will have a genetic mutation that makes them eligible for one of the new "targeted" therapies—drugs that work better than chemo and have fewer side effects. "Because you are a woman and a nonsmoker," says Dr. Dar, "you are more likely to have one of these mutations. It's a small likelihood, maybe 15 percent, but I'm optimistic."

Dr. Dar is threading the needle between realism and hope, a reason for us to keep moving forward. I think all oncologists must do that; it is an important part of the job.

Lynn and I feel tremendous pressure to get going, so when we learn that Roosevelt Hospital can do the biopsy a day earlier than Mount Sinai, we jump at the chance. Each passing day feels precious, and we don't want to miss a single one. We have no idea how many delays lie ahead, nor how insignificant the savings of one day will turn out to be.

꿈

All this time, what we originally thought was the main problem—Lynn's abdominal discomfort—hasn't gone away; in fact, it's worse. Lynn now has pain in her back and in her gut. Dr. Dar prescribes codeine, which seems to help, but like any opiate, it blocks her up, and as the days pass her constipation becomes severe, to the point where she hardly leaves the house.

I go out and buy a sample of every type of constipa-
tion-reliever on the shelf. The laxatives and stool softeners
don't work, so on Friday we try suppositories—no luck—
and then, on Saturday, an enema, something we've never
done before. Almost immediately Lynn stiffens, and after
a few ounces cries out and says we have to stop.

Desperate, we leave messages for both Dr. Dar and
Dr. Weinstein and are tremendously relieved when they
quickly return our calls. They suggest which drugs to take
and encourage us to vastly increase the dose. They don't
completely agree with each other, but we feel supported,
and by late afternoon Lynn has her first bowel movement
in days.

We are starting to realize that this is the deal: You get
the best advice you can, but you have to make the final
choice.

That night Lynn sleeps more soundly, but this just
gets her back to where she was a week ago, tired and achy.
She doesn't leave the apartment on Sunday and shows no
signs of doing so until our next appointment.

On Sunday afternoon, when I write a CaringBridge
post about the weekend, Lynn insists that I leave out the
constipation. "They don't need to know that," she says.
"Just tell them I was uncomfortable, and the doctors were
helpful."

Tuesday, October 7, 2014

We arrive at Roosevelt by 7:30 a.m., having been told that
Lynn will receive the first lung biopsy of the day. Not true.
We soon learn that someone else has been scheduled before

Lynn, and an hour later we get bumped again because of an urgent ICU case.

We're in a large room full of people waiting for outpatient procedures, each in their own curtained alcove. The atmosphere feels jumpy and chaotic. The nurses are busy, it's hard to get answers, and we start to wonder who is in charge. Lynn has had no food or liquid since last night and was told not to take any medication, so she's hungry and her back is killing her.

As the hours pass, her pain increases. One of the nurses apologizes for the delay, saying it's because of the hospital's recent merger into a larger organization. "They're changing our schedules, asking us to do more work in the same amount of time. No one is happy."

This helps explain what we're seeing, but the fact that she shares it with us is disconcerting. I would like to believe that everyone who treats Lynn is in a good mood.

At about 11:30 a.m., they prep Lynn for the procedure and give her some wonderful anesthesia, leaving her pain-free for the first time in a month.

The procedure takes an hour and goes smoothly, but back in the recovery room the drugs wear off and Lynn's pain returns. Other than a small snack and some apple juice, she still isn't allowed to eat. We wait several more hours for them to take an X-ray to confirm that her lung is in no danger of collapsing, then another hour for a radiologist to read it and approve discharge, then another hour for someone to remove the IV.

By the time we finally get out of there, eight and a half hours have passed, and we both have headaches. But at least now the biopsied cells have been sent to the pathology lab; the countdown to start treatment can begin.

～

Nine days crawl by before the radiation therapy.

We spend another half day in the Mount Sinai basement prepping for the procedure, a process called "simulation." A pair of technicians make a plastic mold of Lynn's back to hold her steady during the radiation. They take several CT scans, use markers to write various cryptic symbols on her chest, and give her a small permanent tattoo that they will use next week to target the beam.

Every application of this therapy is individually designed, unique. Initially, Dr. Brown said it would take about four hours to do the planning and twenty minutes to apply the radiation, but after the simulation she tells us that Lynn's tumors are "complicated," and both the planning and the radiation will take longer than she thought.

Lynn asks if the radiation will reduce her back pain. Dr. Brown says yes: "It should start to fade after a few days." But there are no guarantees. "If the pain doesn't resolve, we will regroup and figure out what to do next."

"What would that be?" I ask.

"Probably neurosurgery," she says. "You can't repeat such intensive radiation in the spine. We need to get this right the first time."

The hardest part is having to sit and wait.

I start researching possible treatments, obsessively searching for gold in press releases and cancer websites, even though it is too soon to know what will be useful. I am in my comfort zone, as if preparing for another large project, and while gathering information I can almost forget the sword that hangs over us.

Lynn doesn't work that way. She seeks refuge not in research and planning but in conversations with friends. She is constantly on the phone, talking about almost anything but her cancer, as if she needs reassurance that there is life all around her, that she herself is very much alive.

You can see it in the books we read. I start motoring through Siddhartha Mukherjee's *The Emperor of All Maladies*, a 450-page "biography of cancer," while Lynn loses herself in an immersive historical novel, *The Signature of All Things* by Elizabeth Gilbert, a love story for the natural world.

Lynn never used to watch much TV. She called even the best shows mindless escapism. But now she looks forward to the end of the day when we cuddle together in front of the TV and forget about everything else. It becomes our favorite shared activity.

Thursday, October 9, 2014

Dr. Dar calls with Lynn's formal diagnosis: non-small cell adenocarcinoma, which he calls "nonsmoker's lung cancer." This is not a surprise, but it is scary.

Lynn googles the phrase and reads about cases where only palliative treatment is possible; basically, trying to make you comfortable while you die. I do my own googling and find several posts suggesting that it is possible, if the lung cancer has only spun off one or two tumors, to cut out or radiate those outliers and then use chemo or radiation on the underlying cancer.

Lynn's cancer is "only" in two discrete places in her right lung and two places in her spine, and not in her lymph nodes or anywhere else. If the spinal tumors are dealt with, can the lung cancer be eliminated?

"Unfortunately, it doesn't work like that," explains Dr. Dar. "The cancer is out of the barn. The fact that it is in Lynn's spine means it is also in her bloodstream, traveling around, looking for other places to land. The best we can do is find a treatment that will shrink the tumors and prevent them from seeding elsewhere."

Increasingly, Dr. Dar is finding ways to tell us that Lynn will have stage IV cancer for the rest of her life. Full remission is so rare that it's not worth thinking about. How long she will live is an open question; it depends on luck and the choices we make. The luck is out of our hands, but we feel a heavy responsibility to make the right choices.

Tuesday, October 14, 2014

More than two weeks after we first learned of them, Lynn undergoes intensive radiation to kill her spinal tumors. There is a preliminary CT scan to make sure nothing has changed. Then lots of positioning in the fancy machine, which zaps the tumors with fifteen precisely targeted bursts of radiation from different angles over the course of an hour. Lynn takes a codeine before the procedure and is half-asleep throughout, unaware of when she is zapped or how long each burst lasts.

It is a glorious fall day, so we walk to and from Mount Sinai, about thirty minutes each way. For the first hour or so, Lynn feels terrific. We think perhaps a miracle has occurred. Then the codeine wears off and she discovers the radiation has irritated her back. What had been a dull, persistent ache is now sharp and hot.

On the way home, we pass a fish store and decide to buy a piece of cod for dinner; soothing food that won't irritate Lynn's stomach. By the time we get home, her back is burning, and she feels worse than ever. Lynn has always been the cook in our household, she loves food in all its variety, but tonight cooking is beyond her. She goes straight to bed, where she lies on her back reading *The New Yorker* magazine above her head, the only position in which she feels comfortable.

After an hour I realize that if I don't get moving, we won't have dinner, so I find a simple recipe for baked cod with garlic and lemon breadcrumbs. Somewhat to my surprise, I enjoy making it. By the time Lynn feels good enough to get out of bed, I've got fish and rice ready for both of us and a side dish of broccoli for me. It's a turning point in my relationship with the kitchen, one that will become increasingly useful when Lynn is no longer able to cook.

Over the next few days, Lynn starts feeling better. She has moments, hours, when she feels okay, before the belly or back pain kicks in. She makes it downtown to the opening of a friend's art show, the first time in six weeks she's done anything like that. But mostly, we are on a physical and emotional roller coaster, lurching between periods when Lynn feels good and difficult days when she can barely get out of bed.

"This is scary," I write on CaringBridge. "We had hoped that as the pain from the spinal tumor decreased,

Lynn's belly symptoms would disappear too, but that isn't happening."

A friend refers Lynn to another gastroenterologist who provides a rare bit of good news. "Cancer changes your metabolism in ways that have a profound effect on every part of you," he says, "including your stomach and intestines. There is reason to hope that many of your digestive problems will go away once your cancer is being treated."

ç

Day after day passes with no word about the genetic analysis that will enable us to start treatment.

Every morning we call Dr. Dar's office, and every morning Arlene tells us the same thing: no news yet. Eventually, we give up and stop calling. We have to believe that Arlene will tell us when there is news.

"This is driving us crazy," I write on CaringBridge. "We are anxious to get started before the cancer spreads further."

In the vacuum caused by these delays, I feel desperate to do something, anything, to move the process forward. I'm used to being in control, and the lack of control is indeed driving me crazy.

So we decide to line up a second opinion to see if there is something else we should be doing. I email my contact at Yale, hoping he will recommend an oncologist in New York, but instead he refers us to his colleague Dr. Roy Herbst, head of thoracic oncology at Yale's cancer center, who sends word that he would be happy to see us whenever we're ready.

When I mention Dr. Herbst to Dr. Dar, he gets excited. He knows all about Herbst and speaks of him as if he were a movie star. Apparently, Herbst and his team are on the forefront of some of the most exciting new developments in the treatment of lung cancer.

That night I stay up late, energized and hopeful, googling Dr. Herbst and reading scientific papers about his work. Lynn, however, is not so sure. The more excited I become about Herbst and immunotherapy and the new "PD-1 checkpoint inhibitors," the more it all feels like pie in the sky to her. She is already depressed by constant fatigue and discomfort and not sure we will gain anything by going all the way to Yale—a two-hour drive.

Monday, October 27, 2014

At last! Arlene calls to say that Dr. Dar has received the genetic analysis. I cancel my afternoon plans, and we meet him in his office at 1:30.

Dr. Dar smiles as he rises to greet us. "I have very good news!" he says. "Your tumor tested positive for the EGFR mutation. This means you can take Tarceva, a targeted therapy that is a lot easier on your body than chemo and usually works better and lasts longer."

Rather than an intravenous infusion, Tarceva is a pill that Lynn will take every day. The most common side effects are fatigue, skin rashes, and acne-like pimples.

The bad news is that Tarceva, like all the targeted cancer drugs, doesn't work for everyone. "There's about a 40 percent chance it won't work for you—and even if it does, your cancer will eventually mutate and become resistant to it. Then, we will have to try something else."

"How long will the Tarceva keep working?" asks Lynn.

"It depends," says Dr. Dar. "Sometimes just a few months, but it could be years. I had a patient who was on Tarceva for seven years and then moved to Florida. He was doing fine the last time I saw him. We just have to try it and see what happens."

We've been reluctant to tell Dr. Dar that we want to see Dr. Herbst, but clearly it is now or never. Dr. Dar surprises us by saying he thinks this is a great idea. "If you can get your hands on the good stuff," he says, "you should definitely take it. That's what I would do." And the only place you can get the good stuff—immunotherapy—is at a cancer center like Yale.

When Lynn and I get home we research Tarceva and learn that half the time it either doesn't work or stops working in less than thirteen months. And even when it works, most patients die within a few years. On top of that, the list of potential adverse reactions that Dr. Dar didn't mention is downright scary: lung disease that can kill you, stomach problems that can kill you, and the list goes on and on. But the Tarceva site helpfully points out that chemo is even harder on your body than Tarceva, and that many lung cancer patients on chemo die in a matter of months, not years.

After reading all this Lynn turns to me and says, "This disease is really serious," as if realizing it for the first time.

I sleep poorly that night, and the next morning we start talking about the trade-offs between cancer treatment and quality of life. At what point will Lynn's life be so diminished that there's no point in continuing? How will we know when the side effects are worse than the disease?

Lynn lists her favorite activities: "Painting and drawing, cooking and eating, viewing art, getting exercise,
seeing friends, petting the cats, and being with you." She
smiles. "Not necessarily in that order." But she doesn't
know which of these are truly essential, and how she will
feel if her cancer, or its treatment, takes them away.

"Maybe I can live with less," she says. "Maybe just
being with you is enough."

Until now, Lynn has wanted to take the easier path:
continuing with Dr. Dar and Tarceva. But following this
path will only buy us at most a year or two. Dr. Herbst and
his immunotherapy drugs might give us more with fewer
side effects. So we decide to shoot for "the good stuff" and
make an appointment to see Dr. Herbst as soon as possible, which turns out to be almost two weeks from now.
Nothing about Lynn's treatment is moving as quickly as
we want.

Saturday, November 1, 2014
www.CaringBridge.org/LynnKotula*

We are planning to go up to New Haven by train on Monday afternoon and spend the night in a no-frills hotel
attached to the hospital. From our perspective, everything is riding on these appointments. Even if Lynn is not
eligible for a clinical trial, we need to start meeting and
networking with the doctors who have access to "the
good stuff"—and to the newer varieties of good stuff
that are only now being invented. These are the connections we have, and we're going to push them as far as we
can.

---

* This web address no longer exists. During those years, it was the gateway to
our journal.

Lynn, who has just read this over my shoulder, is emphatic that she is not disabled, and although she is sometimes exhausted and needs to stay close to home, at other times she feels fine and wants to venture forth. In the past week, we've had two dinners and a brunch with friends, and today her cold seems to be fading, so we're planning to go downtown to see some gallery shows.

11 Comments

It's sweet to picture Lynn at your shoulder while you type, so that it feels like this is all coming from both of you. We have to have hope, and we do. —Elizabeth

⏜

Yale New Haven Hospital rises like a spaceship from the surrounding parking lots, and everything there looks modern and high-tech. We follow signs to the cancer center, where the thoracic waiting room is in a large alcove on the side of a corridor which, despite being in the heart of a busy hospital, feels rather intimate. There are a few other patients, but before we can size them up, we are ushered into an empty office where Dr. Herbst joins us.

Highly credentialed, affiliated with just about every branch of the Yale medical establishment, and chair of its Thoracic Oncology department, Dr. Herbst looks every inch the senior figure he is. His manner is low-key and solicitous. He introduces himself and asks how Lynn is feeling and confirms that Tarceva is indeed the drug of choice for her. Then he pauses to make sure he has our full attention.

"There is another option," he says. "We're running a clinical trial here that we think might work for you. We're testing one of the new immunotherapy drugs in combination with Tarceva. You would take both of them together."

I glance sideways at Lynn; we didn't expect this. There's electricity in the air as Dr. Herbst continues.

"While each of these therapies has less than a 100 percent success rate on its own, we hope taking them together will increase the chance that you respond to at least one of them. And if the immunotherapy works, it could beat the cancer into remission for a very long time." As an added bonus, the clinical trial will pay for Lynn's Tarceva, which will save us thousands of dollars in co-payments.

This is perfect, even better than we had dared hope: Lynn will get the proven benefits of Tarceva, plus the "good stuff" on top of it. I am practically jumping with excitement until Dr. Herbst adds that there is one catch: all of the procedures have to be in New Haven, a four-hour round trip from our apartment. You can't be in the trial at Yale and get the drugs in New York.

"Can you commit to that?" he asks.

"How many visits are we talking about?" Lynn says.

To our surprise, Dr. Herbst isn't sure. This is not one of "his" studies; he only knows the outline. He leaves us saying he will find someone who can answer our questions, and that's the last we see of him.

A few minutes later, a "study nurse" comes in with a thick binder that she opens on the desk in front of her. As she reads from it, Lynn grows pale: We will need to be here at least three days in a row next week for scans, tests, and a lung biopsy. Then at least two visits the following week, including a second lung biopsy. Thereafter, a full-day visit each week with intravenous infusions of the immunotherapy drug every few visits, and then another biopsy, and more tests . . . The pattern doesn't settle down to "only" one day at the hospital every three weeks until week ten of the trial, and then it continues like that for two years or until the drugs stop working, whichever comes first.

Clearly, the logistics are horrible; it sounds exhausting even without the stress of traveling back and forth and spending so many nights in a hotel. We ask if the same study is being done in New York, and the nurse surprises us by not knowing the answer, though she agrees it's a good idea for us to find out. She makes no move to do this herself, perhaps she's not allowed to, but she turns the computer to face us and waits while I google the name of the immunotherapy drug.

Immediately, I get a hit on the Sloan Kettering website, where a study is underway that sounds a lot like the one in New Haven. But it doesn't say whether they're accepting new patients.

Websites can be out of date, and we don't want to walk away from our precious slot at Yale until we are sure we can get one in New York.

"Can you call your counterpart at Sloan Kettering and find out for us?" I ask.

She shakes her head. "I wouldn't know who to call. It's up to you to make whatever calls you need to make." She hands us a twenty-eight-page consent form and leaves us to it.

Our heads are spinning. We came to New Haven for guidance and support, and instead find ourselves trying to navigate the healthcare system almost entirely on our own.

The morning is half gone, so we head downstairs to the large cafeteria on the first floor, where there is good cell service and strong coffee. We set up an office on a couple of chairs in a back corner and spend the next few hours working our cell phones.

After several false starts, we get a message to Dr. Charles Rudin, the doctor who leads the study at Sloan Kettering, and thirty minutes later we hear from his assistant that there are indeed a few openings in the study. But before they will even talk to Lynn, she needs to make an in-person appointment with Dr. Rudin or one of his colleagues. And before Lynn can do that, she needs to talk to a new patient gatekeeper who, when we finally reach one, tells us that they need copies of all of Lynn's test results and consultation reports before she can even consider making an appointment.

Another round of phone calls to Dr. Dar and Mt. Sinai, and by some minor miracle we get the test results faxed to Sloan Kettering while we nervously eat our lunch.

In the middle of all this, Dr. Steve Gore stops by, my friend-of-a-friend who is head of medical oncology at Yale New Haven. Steve thinks we're doing the right thing getting into a clinical trial. "Patients enrolled in trials tend to have better outcomes than those who don't participate," he tells us, "even when the drugs don't work for them. I think it's because of the intensive monitoring and testing that is done in a trial."

He then adds that there would be a real benefit to doing the trial in New York rather than New Haven. "If Lynn has a severe reaction to the immunotherapy drug, relatively few doctors will understand what is happening, and she will want to be as close to them as possible."

This is a grim possibility that we hadn't considered.

When we tell Steve that we hope to get an appointment with Charles Rudin at Sloan Kettering, his face lights up: "Charlie! We used to work together at Johns Hopkins. He's a great guy. You'll really like him."

Then we tell Steve that there are only twenty-six patients in the study nationwide, and he says, "Oh, that's really small. You don't want to miss your chance."

By this point, I am excited about doing the clinical trial in New York, but the afternoon keeps dragging on. At about 4:00 p.m., we give up and walk back to the train station. We can always return tomorrow if Sloan Kettering doesn't work out.

It isn't until we are stepping onto the commuter train that my phone rings and Sloan Kettering's gatekeeper confirms that she has received everything she needs. We find a pair of seats in the back of the crowded carriage as I continue talking with her, trying to keep my voice down.

The gatekeeper offers an appointment with Dr. Rudin, but it is three weeks away. Lynn is desperate to start treatment, so we ask whether there is anyone else who can see her sooner. After a pause, she offers us an appointment with Dr. Matthew Hellmann, who can see Lynn next week.

As our train speeds through the Connecticut countryside, I look up Dr. Hellmann on the Sloan Kettering website. He is young, one of the more junior members of the department, but the study we want is listed on his web

page, he trained at some of the best hospitals in the country—and he has a nice smile.

Dr. Hellmann on the Sloan Kettering website

ᔓ

We are starting to realize that both Yale and Sloan Kettering
are big organizations with lots of rules and hoops you
must jump through, where you spend most of your time
talking to people other than the doctors. This is quite a
change from our direct connection with Dr. Dar and his
nurse, Arlene.

Lynn and I talk about this over dinner. It occurs to
me that because we haven't spoken directly with Dr.
Hellmann, Lynn's appointment might appear in his calendar as just a routine consultation.

"What if he isn't the right person to talk to, or can't
get you into the trial, or doesn't want to? We need him to
understand that the whole point of the appointment is to

get you into the clinical trial, and if this can be done more quickly by some other route, we should take that route."

"Yes," agrees Lynn. "And if Sloan Kettering isn't going to work out, we need to know right away, so I can call New Haven while they still have an opening." We are willing to endure all those trips to New Haven if it is the only way for her to have a shot at "the good stuff."

First thing in the morning, Lynn speaks with Dr. Hellmann's assistant, Andres, a sweet man with a middle-European accent. She tells Andres that the famous Dr. Roy Herbst has offered her a slot in the trial in New Haven, and we need to know ASAP if it will be possible to do it in New York instead. We can't afford to wait another week.

A few minutes later, Andres calls back. "Dr. Hellmann is very interested," he says. "He would like to see you today. Although he is fully booked, he can squeeze you in sometime this afternoon."

Later we will learn that it is quite difficult to get people to sign up for intensive clinical trials, and institutions like Yale and Sloan Kettering scramble to find patients willing to do them. But at the time, we think we are chasing a scarce resource that might disappear any minute. We hang up the phone giddy with excitement.

We still have a few hours, so we decide to walk the several miles to Sloan's outpatient pavilion, through the heart of Central Park. We love those walks to the hospitals, as they breathe life into what would otherwise be a more sterile experience: a parade of waiting rooms and examination rooms and anonymous Formica-covered offices. Inhaling the fragrant autumn air, we can almost forget where we are going and why we need to be there.

The Gingko trees have dropped their leaves overnight, and the grass is newly covered by a spongy carpet of gold.

Wednesday, November 5, 2014

Sloan's outpatient pavilion occupies the bottom half of an office building on East 53rd Street in a business district we usually avoid. As we enter the lobby, a jovial doorman calls out "Good afternoon!" to everyone who walks in. Although this is his job, he seems to mean it. In future visits, we will look forward to seeing him and feel disappointed when we don't.

There is an upholstered bench in the elevator in case you need to sit down, and when the doors open on the sixth floor, we are greeted by two smiling young women who check in new arrivals. Like the doorman in the lobby, they seem to have no other job.

Painted on the walls beside the check-in desk are the names of the doctors in Sloan's Thoracic Oncology department, more than two dozen of them, divided into those who provide medical treatment (the oncologists) and a separate group of surgeons. I quickly find Dr. Hellmann's name among the oncologists. This feels reassuring.

The waiting room is huge, especially compared to the ones at Yale New Haven and Mount Sinai. The air feels steamy because the room is full of people. I spot a few individuals sitting alone, but most are in groups of two or three: husbands and wives, older men and women accompanied by one or both of their adult children.

Everyone is waiting for an appointment with an oncologist, and everyone either has lung cancer or is with someone who does.

We find a pair of seats and spend the afternoon sur-
reptitiously observing them. It is a cross section of young
and old, well dressed and well worn, multiple ethnicities
and languages. There are people who look healthy, while
others are desperately thin and pale. Some use a cane and
lean against a chair or walker, others stand and chat near
the coffee machine, or slump in wheelchairs with their
eyes closed. A few carry personal oxygen tanks in back-
packs or shoulder bags or pulled behind them on little
wheels.

Periodically, one of the cheerful, young employees
weaves through the room calling out someone's name, but
as the hours pass they never ask for Lynn.

Our neighbors on the couch change over, and for a
while we strike up a conversation with a married couple from Virginia Beach, both in their sixties, the woman
apparently healthy and cheerful while her husband grips
her hand tightly. It turns out that she is the patient. She
received several cycles of chemo at her local hospital, but
it isn't working, so they arranged for a second opinion at
Sloan Kettering and drove up yesterday. Now they, like us,
are waiting to see their doctor for the first time.

In coming months, they will be on the same cycle of
Wednesday visits as Lynn, and she will run into them several times. With each encounter, the woman seems to fade
a little. After a few months, she starts using portable oxygen, and then one day Lynn realizes that she hasn't seen
them in a long time. They disappear from her life as so
many cancer patients will—from the waiting room, from
the support group meetings—leaving her to wonder what
happened and to assume the worst.

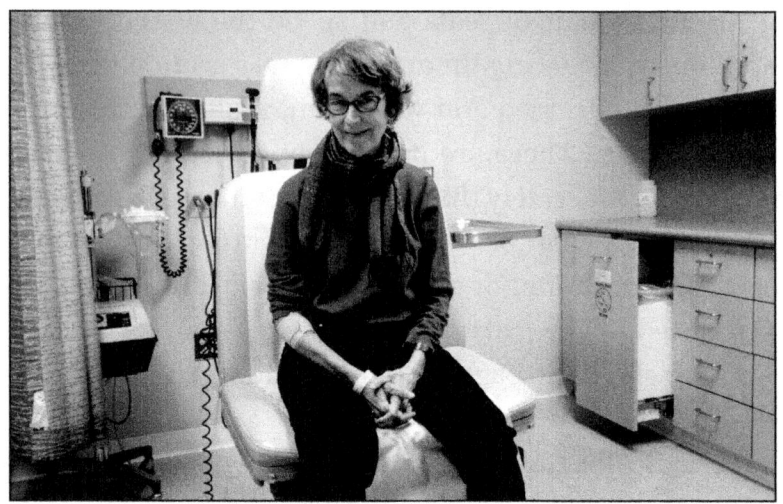

Waiting to meet Dr. Hellmann, November 5, 2014

Late in the afternoon we are ushered into a salmon-pink exam room, where we finally meet Dr. Hellmann. While Dr. Herbst radiated white-coat confidence, Dr. Hellmann is young, rumpled, and self-effacing, and there is a softness about him that suggests he has little time for exercise. As he enters the room, he apologizes for the four-hour delay but says this is the sort of thing we can expect at Sloan Kettering: There are just too many patients trying to use too few facilities here.

He pulls up a small rolling chair and plants it directly in front of Lynn, close enough to touch her knee.

"I understand you were in New Haven yesterday," he says. "How did that go?"

Lynn tells him about Dr. Herbst and the clinical trial, saying that we hope to get into the same trial in New York.

"We can do that," says Dr. Hellmann, and we both breathe a sigh of relief. "You just have to decide if you really want it."

Dr. Hellmann is thorough and patient. He looks Lynn in the eye as he slowly reviews the trial in detail: the drugs Lynn will take, the procedures involved, the potential side effects. His tone is gentle, reassuring. "If anything starts to go wrong," he promises, "you will be able to drop out of the trial and revert to just taking Tarceva, as you would have with Dr. Dar."

Then he hands us a fat binder, the trial's bible, and leaves us to decide whether we want to proceed.

Alone in the exam room, Lynn and I have a difficult conversation. I urge her to sign up: "This is our best chance to beat the odds and win back a few more years of life."

But Lynn keeps circling back to the downsides. "I'm scared," she says, again and again. Scared of spending so much time at the hospital, scared of the two painful lung biopsies, scared of all the needle sticks and blood draws, and scared of the horrific side effects from those two powerful drugs, which occupy several pages of the binder.

"The side effects are just possibilities," I reply, "they don't happen to everyone. The cancer is real and eating you up as we speak. Unless we do something drastic, you probably won't be alive a year from now."

It feels like a tug-of-war: I strain to drag Lynn forward, inch by inch, toward the only treatment that offers real hope, but progress is slow and her fear powerful. It takes a lot of effort for me to remain calm and patient with the woman I love.

In the end, it is the escape hatch that makes the difference: Lynn can leave the trial at any time. As this option sinks in, she relaxes and stops resisting. I find Dr. Hellmann and tell him she is ready to sign.

On the way out, we spend an hour with a young man whose entire job seems to be scheduling appointments. By the time he finishes planning Lynn's next two weeks, it is nearly 7:00 p.m. The waiting room has emptied, and both he and we are dying to go home, so we don't question him as he plows through all the different tests and meetings and procedures that Lynn is required to undergo. Eventually, he hands us a small stack of paper, several pages for each of the events he has scheduled, and when we get home, it takes us an hour to copy them into Lynn's calendar.

Switching to Sloan Kettering means we will have to say goodbye to Dr. Dar and his wonderful nurse, Arlene, who jumped through hoops for us again and again. But there can only be one oncologist in charge of Lynn's treatment, and for now that is Dr. Hellmann. Lynn feels guilty about this and decides to bring Arlene a bouquet of flowers in the morning.

That night, I spend hours writing a CaringBridge post describing the twists and turns of the last two days.

"Wow, Lynn and Tony, you've been moving mountains while on the roller coaster!" responds our friend Susan.

"After reading all these posts, I totally want the two of you to run my life," writes Ann. "You get so much done!"

Lynn smiles when she reads these and writes one of her rare comments: "It's Tony who gets the credit for his dogged pursuit on my behalf and his incredible organizational skills. (Why can't we apply those to more mundane tasks like keeping an orderly household?)"

~

Sunday, November 9, 2014
www.CaringBridge.org/LynnKotula

We're back in waiting mode while Lynn takes all the tests that are required by the clinical trial.

As far as I can tell, we are in the best possible spot. Lynn, however, doesn't feel this way at all. For her, this is a scary time. Her discomforts worsen by the day, and she wonders what the side effects will be like, how will they differ from what she's feeling now, and if she'll feel any better during the trial.

We had some lovely conversations over the past few weeks, but today she said she just can't get there as her thoughts turn inward to her body. She has changed to a low-fiber diet and is managing to keep her weight steady, so compared to the people we saw in Sloan Kettering's waiting room on Wednesday, she's doing great. But she can't help wondering, Is this the best I'm going to feel for the next two years—or forever?

8 comments

It's tiring to have waiting be such a major part of your lives. What stamina you both have & what a gift you are to each other. —Libby

That night we review the schedule and see that next Thursday we are supposed to meet the interventional radiologist who will perform Lynn's two lung biopsies. Thursday seems far away, so in the morning Lynn calls the radiology office to ask why she needs this meeting.

"So Dr. Erinjeri can explain to you what happens during the biopsy," comes the response. "After that he will schedule your procedure."

This is infuriating. "I just had a lung biopsy last month," says Lynn. "I don't need someone to explain it to me. Can't we skip the meeting and schedule it right away?"

"No, we can't," he says. "That's the procedure and it can't be changed."

As the day passes, we become increasingly annoyed. All the other pieces are in place, but Lynn is required to have this biopsy before she can start treatment. She calls Dr. Erinjeri's assistant again to ask when it might happen, and he says that Dr. Erinjeri is heavily booked, so even after our meeting on Thursday, it will be several weeks before he can perform the procedure.

"Is there someone else who can do it sooner?" asks Lynn.

"Yes, several," says the assistant. "But we can't make that change until you meet with Dr. Erinjeri on Thursday."

This is nuts! Livid, Lynn hangs up and calls Andres, Dr. Hellmann's assistant, and dumps the whole story on him. She tells him that the delay is unacceptable. "You need to fix this scheduling problem. It shouldn't be up to us to do it. And if you can't fix this, we can go back to New Haven. They promised that they can get it all done in less than a week!"

The next morning Andres calls to say he has found another radiologist who can perform the biopsy next week.

"Andres is a miracle worker!" exclaims Lynn, as she puts down her phone. I think it more likely that his power comes from understanding the rules of the clinical trial and its importance to Sloan, and then using Lynn's presence in it to get higher-priority treatment—and perhaps that is a miracle after all.

Tuesday, November 11, 2014
www.CaringBridge.org/LynnKotula

Compared to all the places we've been so far, Sloan Kettering is the most regimented. They have a protocol for everything, from which they won't deviate. You're a widget in their machine. It's a fantastic machine, and many of the people working there are quite nice, but you are still moving through a well-oiled machine.

Part of our task is learning our way around the institution. In hindsight, it was a mistake to take that initial schedule at face value. But it was after 5:30 p.m., and we were exhausted and mistakenly thought the scheduler was giving us the earliest possible appointments. Had we called back the next morning and spoken with Lynn's new treatment team about that crazy schedule, we could've sorted this all out with less agita.

When we meet the radiologist, he seems unbearably young, a near-child who only recently moved here from Beirut. This is one of the problems with growing older: All your doctors start to look like children. But when Lynn asks whether he's performed this procedure before, Dr. Muellam assures her that he's done "at least a thousand" of them, and that Lynn's will be straightforward: "Your tumor is large enough that it will be easy to find, and in a location that poses no particular problems."

Lynn being Lynn, she asks Dr. Muellam to name his favorite Lebanese restaurant in New York. "Almayass," he says without hesitation, "where my favorite dishes are Mouhammara and Queen's Delight."

Lynn beams. She won't be able to eat there herself—she has permanently lost her ability to eat spicy food—but she can still imagine the textures and flavors, and I know she is back on track.

Saturday, November 15, 2014
www.CaringBridge.org/LynnKotula

I am starting to realize that no matter how many appointments I go to with Lynn, no matter how often we talk about her treatment, plan next steps, and worry about what might come thereafter, she is on a journey that I can't fully share. This is usually when I break down and start crying.

A friend heard about the cancer and sent Lynn a short email with a wonderful image. She explained that in her Tai Chi group, "We carry tigers for people when they are going through challenges. The tiger figures as one's challenges or the challenges of one's friends... and if you carry a tiger for someone, you are lifting their load. The three gestures of scooping low, embracing the tiger, and putting the tiger upon the mountain are illustrative of the difference that perspective makes. A tiger is not so terrifying if it is far away on the top of a mountain peak. In fact, it becomes small and manageable there."

Lynn wrote back to thank her friend, and asked if the friend would carry some tigers for her, and also, if the friend could perhaps teach Lynn how to carry tigers.

Then she sat down at her computer and started researching lung cancer support groups.

"I want to carry a tiger for LYNN AND TONY," writes our friend Nancy, who also has stage IV cancer. "And I'll have one for myself, too."

I reply to Nancy, "Everyone who reads these posts is helping us carry the tiger."

In Treatment

We spend the morning at Sloan Kettering, where Lynn has her baseline lung biopsy for the clinical trial. Once again, she will lie in a CT scanner while Dr. Muellam inserts a needle into her lung and takes snippets of the larger tumor. There will be another biopsy next week, so they can compare it to this one and see what a week of Tarceva has done to the lung tumor *before* they hit it with the immunotherapy drug.

In terms of surroundings and workflow, everything goes smoothly this time. Sloan's Outpatient Procedures area is comfortable and well-staffed; she is called into surgery exactly on time, and for the most part, I am able to stay by her side. But Lynn has been anxious all weekend, and when they don't give her enough of the anesthesia, she hears every little thing: the doctor and researchers talking to each other; each "click" as they take snips of the tumor, someone saying "oops." Even worse, because they think she's fully sedated, no one talks to her. There is no "now, we're going to do this" or "now, we're going to do that," and instead all their chatter is with each other, as if she weren't there, much less the most important person in the room.

About halfway through the procedure, she starts to cry, and she continues to feel extremely vulnerable for the next two hours as we wait for the X-rays that will prove her lung hasn't collapsed.

Immediately after the procedure, Dr. Muellam comes into the corridor and apologizes because he realized belatedly that they should have given Lynn more anesthesia, so she wouldn't be aware of what they were saying, or if she did hear it, wouldn't care. "Each patient's reaction to the drugs is different," he says. "I promise that next week we will do better."

He's very nice about it, but he's also very young. I'm not sure he realizes how important this is, or how terrible Lynn feels.

Wednesday, November 19, 2014

More than seven weeks after we first learned of the tumors, Lynn begins treatment for lung cancer. The process eats the whole day. We arrive at Sloan's outpatient pavilion at 10:15 a.m. and don't leave until 6:15 p.m., when they draw one last vial of Lynn's blood. Apparently, every visit to the outpatient center will include these sorts of delays.

In the terminology of a clinical trial, it is Day 1 of Cycle 1. For the next ten weeks, Lynn will see Dr. Hellmann, have her blood drawn, and vital signs taken every Wednesday; after that, she will "only" need to go every three weeks, plus additional visits for scans and tests, of which there will be many.

Generally, each cycle will begin with an infusion of the experimental immunotherapy drug. This week, though, Lynn will take Tarceva on its own for seven days before her first immunotherapy infusion. The doctors hope that taking Tarceva first will "rough up" her tumors and make the miracle drug more effective.

In the morning we meet with Dr. Hellmann, which gives us a chance to ask him the tough questions that occurred to us after we saw him last week. It's amazing how hard it is to think of every question during those precious minutes when your doctor is with you. Going forward, Lynn will prepare a list of questions before each visit, so this doesn't happen again.

Dr. Hellmann sits close to Lynn and engages her directly. He isn't as effusively warm as Dr. Dar, and I can't imagine him hugging her as Dr. Dar did, but the more he talks, the more I like him.

Dr. Hellmann says that although it is possible the tumors have been growing slowly in Lynn's lungs for years, if we do nothing, she will die in a matter of months, not years.

There is no guarantee that the two drugs together (Tarceva and the immunotherapy) will work better than either on its own. But when dealing with other diseases, including HIV, researchers have found that the best approach is to hit them with a combination of drugs right from the start. That is what the clinical trial aims to test.

"How will we know that it's working?" asks Lynn.

"Because you'll feel better. The scans can provide confirmation that something good is happening, but they will come weeks after the fact. The most important indicator is how you feel."

"And how will we know which drug is doing it?"

"We won't," says Dr. Hellmann. "If the treatment succeeds, there will be no way to know whether one or the other drug is doing most of the work."

When Lynn's tumors stop responding to the drugs, as they most surely will, it will probably be because the cancer has developed a secondary mutation. When that happens, she might be lucky enough to target the mutation with a different drug. "There are many new drugs being developed specifically for this purpose," he says. "Perhaps one of them will be ready by the time you need it. We'll walk this road together, and I'll be with you every step of the way."

I like hearing this, but Lynn thinks it sounds corny. She's the one doing the walking, after all.

At 2:00 p.m., a nurse brings Lynn her first bottle of thirty Tarceva pills, and Lynn swallows one under the nurse's watchful eye. Then she spends the afternoon being closely observed, her vital signs taken every hour to see how well her body tolerates the medication. This is the same pill that Lynn would've taken at home had we remained with Dr. Dar, in which case no one would have paid her this kind of attention. Patients in clinical trials really are under a spotlight. Today, it feels a bit intrusive; later we will both come to treasure the attention.

As the hours pass, Lynn is on pins and needles, wondering whether each little twinge or cough is significant. She knows this is highly unlikely after just one pill, but it's not easy to turn off one's hopes and fears.

In the end, nothing seems to happen, and Lynn leaves the building feeling much as she did when we arrived. Even so, we are both in a good mood. It really is a relief to have started treatment.

⌒

Each morning Lynn takes Tarceva immediately after waking, then waits an hour before she can eat breakfast. For two days, they don't seem to do anything, but on Friday she floats into my office shaking her head.

"I think the Tarceva is working," she says. "It's amazing. I feel like myself for the first time in . . ." But she can't finish the sentence because she doesn't remember when that was.

That night I write a post to tell our friends, and they respond with cheers and encouragement.

"Wonderful! So glad to hear that things are looking up," says Petey.

"Hooray for progress!" says Ann.

"Wow! Sounds like the worst is over!" says Maria.

You'd think these comments would make us feel good but reading them disturbs us. At breakfast the next day, we try to figure out why. Any way you look at it, this is good news: The Tarceva is working, Lynn's stomach is calm, her pain is down. Why can't we relax and enjoy it?

Saturday, November 22, 2014
www.CaringBridge.org/LynnKotula

Lynn and I have been feeling uncomfortable this morning and trying to figure out why. Yes, she does feel much better than three days ago, and when she ventured out into the world to drop off a painting at her gallery, she ran into lots of friends who said, "Wow, you look great!"—which she does. But she still has back pain, stomach issues, low energy, and her diet is extremely limited.

Emotionally, Lynn's ground is shifting. The severe pain is gone, and it seems the cancer is not going to get her this year—great! But she is entering a state-of-being commonly called "living with cancer," which in her case means "living with incurable cancer." This is more than just a physical condition.

We know the Tarceva is doing something good, so we hope that Lynn will feel increasingly better as it shrinks her tumors and reduces her pain. But we're told that side effects can show up at any time, and Lynn is constantly, nervously on the lookout for them. Worse is the knowledge that, on its own, Tarceva only works for an average of thirteen months. Unless the immunotherapy turns out to be a miracle drug, the cancer will come back at some point.

Lots of people learn to live with incurable diseases. One friend has been living with an incurable cancer for years and has posted many supportive comments here. Another has advanced ALS, which has already taken her mobility and is expected to take her life soon. Both are living life fully. I guess they have each found a way to make peace with the constant underlying fear. Now it's Lynn's turn. She and I have had some wonderful times as a direct result of her illness, spending so many days together and taking lovely walks through the park. We don't always, or even usually, have heavy conversations. But every moment together is heightened, more precious, than just two months ago. And I expect that will remain the case even when her treatment becomes routine, and we stop spending so much time together.

My friend with ALS called this morning because she has trouble reading long posts. Lynn and I love talking to her; she is ahead of us in this journey. I told her about Lynn's response to the Tarceva. "That's great news," she said. "You have a cushion now. You can relax and breathe. Then, eventually, it will be time to wrap your cloak around you and walk into the wind again."

When Lynn reads what I've drafted, it makes her uncomfortable. "This whole thing is about how it feels to have cancer," she says. "But I don't want to 'be cancer' to my friends. That's not what defines me. It's just a condition, and we're starting to find out what that means."

So I add her words to the end of the post, and she gives me permission to publish it.

> *9 Comments*
>
> *There's no way this cancer defines Lynn or changes our love &*
> *admiration for her.* —Libby
>
> *These posts have exactly the opposite effect: They dispel the one-*
> *sided "being cancer" picture.* —Mark

Every Monday evening I spend ninety minutes with my friend Sue, who has ALS.

Sue and I met in college and later moved into the same neighborhood; we occasionally bumped into each other on the street. One day last year, she was sitting in a wheelchair at the local pizzeria, so I asked, "Sue, why are you in that wheelchair?"

"I have ALS," she announced, as if that were a good thing.

"Well, that sucks."

She grinned. "Tell me about it."

I asked Sue whether there was anything I could do for her, and to my surprise she said yes: "I need someone to help with correspondence and bill paying. I'm losing control of my fingers, and it's only going to get worse." We agreed that I would stop by once a week.

When Sue was diagnosed, her doctor said that a patient with her flavor of ALS usually lives for five more years. This is exactly what happened to Sue. She tried everything she could—multiple doctors, two clinical trials—but nothing slowed its progress.

I was with Sue for three of those years. She somehow remained cheerful and optimistic, hosting gatherings of friends in her apartment and, once, a chamber music concert, with only an occasional burst of anger or depression. She showed me how to live gracefully in the face of a fatal disease.

Lynn, too, wanted to learn from Sue. After each visit, Lynn debriefed me, asking what Sue had been up to that week, how she was coping, as if seeking reassurance that when her turn comes, she, too, will be able to cope.

When I told Sue about Lynn's cancer, she gasped out loud, as if the tragedy were hers, and from then on she was terribly concerned about Lynn and frequently gave us useful advice. She was greatly relieved when I said that I intended to continue visiting on Mondays, that she wasn't going to lose me to Lynn's disease.

Clearly, I had become an important part of Sue's life. And she, by lighting the way forward, was becoming an increasingly important part of ours.

Tuesday, November 25, 2014

We are back at Sloan Kettering for the second needle biopsy.

All weekend Lynn has been nervous about this procedure, remembering how badly she felt during the first one. But almost as soon as we arrive, the intake nurse tells us that there is a notation on the board to make sure Lynn receives plenty of sedation today, a reassuring reminder that Sloan Kettering is an impressive place. Then, just before the procedure, Dr. Muellam meets with us and reviews what happened last week. "Today will be better," he says. "I promise, you won't hear anything."

This pleases Lynn, and when they start to wheel her away, she smiles and squeezes my hand, as if to reassure us both that she will be okay.

Immediately after the procedure, Dr. Muellam calls my cell phone to say that everything went well. Lynn seemed more relaxed today, so they decided to give her the same amount of medication as last week.

When I see Lynn a few minutes later, she is still groggy, dozing lightly. As she comes out of it, she says, "The drugs worked much better this time! I didn't feel a thing." She is surprised when I tell her that the dose was the same. I think the main difference must be Lynn's state of mind. Last week everything was scary and unknown; she hadn't started taking Tarceva and didn't know whether it would work. This week she went in feeling much better, both physically and mentally, because she knows the Tarceva is working. As a result the anesthesia worked better, too.

We leave the hospital in a good mood, and since the weather is mild we walk all the way home through Central Park, holding hands most of the way. We marvel at how many colors remain on the trees after the most vivid leaves have fallen. We take pictures of some bright red Hawthorn berries that contrast sharply with the brown branches behind them.

The next day Lynn receives her first dose of MPDL3280A, the experimental drug that offers the possibility of a miracle cure. It is also my birthday, a nice coincidence and the perfect birthday present.

Once again we spend the whole day at Sloan's outpatient facility, arriving at 10:15 a.m. and leaving just after 8:00 p.m., including a two-hour break when Lynn is allowed out for lunch.

The day was supposed to be shorter, but before they can give Lynn her treatment they have to draw blood to make sure her levels are normal, and then we meet with Dr. Hellmann and his nurse, Maureen. The blood draw is easy, but we lose two hours waiting for Dr. Hellmann and become increasingly annoyed because we know that seven hours of treatment lie ahead. Last week, we only waited fifteen minutes to see Dr. Hellmann, same time of day, same day of week. You can't predict this stuff. But Dr. Hellmann did tell us that long delays would be common.

Then it's time for the Tarceva, a mandatory two hour gap to absorb it, the intravenous infusion of the miracle drug into Lynn's arm, and more waiting to make sure she doesn't react badly (anaphylactic shock, anyone?) as they check her vital signs every fifteen minutes.

Lynn is assigned to a private infusion room with a comfortable reclining chair and two somewhat less comfortable visitor chairs. We hang out there for almost four hours, talking with the nurses about their experiences both here and at other hospitals. One young nurse, in particular, is quite chatty; I think he was assigned to pay special attention to us, since this is Lynn's first infusion. The conversation is surprisingly pleasant, though the topics include powerful side effects, bone marrow transplants, hypochondria (his, not his patients'), drug addiction, and death. Just talking in such a matter-of-fact way about the reality of other people's lives feels liberating, anxiety-reducing.

Lynn has no reaction to the infusion, or at least none that we can tell. It might as well be water. But from the intensity with which they observe her, it's clear that immunotherapy is powerful stuff.

My mother lives a mile from Sloan's outpatient facility, so during the two-hour gap we decide to visit her. She is thrilled when we say we'd like to bring a sandwich for lunch but less thrilled—stunned, even—when we tell her Lynn has stage IV cancer that has metastasized to her spine.

For weeks I've worried about this moment, but the conversation goes surprisingly well. Lynn is sitting right there, looking healthy and full of life, and we quickly add that the drugs are working. My mother doesn't ask why we took so long to tell her; she wants to know what will happen next.

"We're really lucky!" says Lynn, with just the right amount of enthusiasm. "I'm in a clinical trial at Memorial Sloan Kettering. They're testing a brand new immuno-therapy drug that could completely kill the tumors. I'll have my first infusion this afternoon."

Shirley loves hearing this: We are on the cutting edge of science, and she is a great believer in science. We share as much as we can about Lynn's diagnosis and treatment, omitting only the grim statistics, the likelihood that this cancer can't be cured. Details she doesn't need to know.

"Just keep me informed," she says, as we stand up to leave. "That's all I ask. I won't be able to sleep if I don't know."

"Of course, I will, Mom. Whatever happens, you'll be the first to know."

It feels terrible to lie to my mother, but this is one promise I can't possibly keep.

∽

Over the next few days, Lynn's energy grows. We enjoy a small Thanksgiving dinner with friends, and on Saturday we walk to Lynn's studio for the first time in months, climbing together to the top floor, planning to set things up so she can start a new painting.

But when we open the door, Lynn is dismayed to see wet plaster drooping from the ceiling and water stains on the Masonite that protects the floor. She speaks with the managing agent about repairing the roof, but this involves clearing out the space, which means she won't be able to resume painting anytime soon.

Making art is essential to Lynn; she needs to draw or paint to get through the day. While the studio is unavailable, she draws at home, filling dozens of notebooks with pencil sketches of me and our cat, Jack, who sleeps constantly and is happy to pose whenever she needs.

"Cat 1"

Wednesday, December 3, 2014

For the first time, Lynn feels secure enough to go to her weekly meeting with Dr. Hellmann on her own.

Dr. Hellmann tells her that when they analyzed Lynn's second biopsy after seven days on Tarceva but before she started the immunotherapy drug, a significant number of the tumor cells had already died. "You're not feeling better because you're imagining it," he says. "The Tarceva is demonstrably killing the cancer cells."

Lynn starts going out again, meeting friends at galleries and museums, and everyone tells her how good she looks. Afterwards, she comes home and collapses, but they don't know that. Her friends see her the way they always have, not as a cancer patient.

Before long she develops an itchy rash, a common side effect of Tarceva: spots and blotches on her arms, shoulders, and face. The rash is a piece of cake compared to the side effects of traditional chemo, so we aren't complaining.

Dr. Hellmann's nurse, Maureen, suggests some over-the-counter topical creams. These work for a few weeks, but then the rash becomes more widespread and annoying, so Dr. Hellmann refers Lynn to Sloan Kettering's chief dermatologist, a dapper man named Mario Lacouture.

Dr. Lacouture wears tailored suits and soft leather moccasins and calls Lynn "lovely lady" every time he sees her. Lynn loves this; it makes her feel special, though she assumes he does the same for all his female patients. He prescribes a series of stronger remedies that are more effective, though the rash continues to come and go for as long as Lynn takes Tarceva.

But that's not the worst side effect.

"It's not the cancer that's killing me, it's the diarrhea," says Lynn one morning. Then she makes me promise not to quote her, since friends don't always appreciate it when she jokes about cancer.

Now that Lynn is no longer in constant pain, she has stopped taking codeine, which means she is no longer constipated. But it turns out that both Tarceva and the MPDL can cause diarrhea, which in Lynn's case they do. It comes on powerfully and unpredictably.

We're out to dinner with our friend Kathy when Lynn suddenly excuses herself and threads between tables to the bathroom. I sit with Kathy making small talk, which becomes increasingly difficult as the minutes pass.

When Lynn returns her pants are wet. "I didn't make it to the toilet," she explains. "I spent most of that time washing my pants in the sink and cleaning up the bathroom." She doesn't meet our eyes.

"Don't worry about it," says Kathy. "It happens." Kathy is a cancer survivor; she understands.

The diarrhea isn't constant, and Lynn isn't chained to the toilet, but the possibility of an event is omnipresent. This wouldn't be a problem if she were still staying home, but now she wants to be out and about almost every day.

Lynn carries pre-opened Loperamide (Imodium) pills at all times. They are individually packaged and require scissors to open. Apparently, the drug company assumes you will only take them at home, which is a real problem when you're desperately fumbling for one in public.

Lynn has to worry each morning: "How does my gut feel? Can I safely go out?" Diarrhea is an inherent side effect of Tarceva, so she can expect to have this problem for as long as she continues taking the drug. Which probably means for the rest of her life.

Lynn is well aware that this is a small problem compared to the alternatives, but she doesn't directly experience her cancer, so the possibility of diarrhea looms much larger in our day to day activities.

The Loperamide instructions say to wait until you have an episode before taking one, but after the disastrous incident in the restaurant, Lynn decides that isn't good enough. She gets Dr. Hellmann's permission to start taking them before leaving the apartment, clogging herself in advance, and then to ignore the limit for how many of them you are supposed to take in a day. This strategy works much better.

Monday, December 7, 2015
www.CaringBridge.org/LynnKotula

One of the problems with being told by oncologists, "If you feel good, don't worry," is that when you don't feel good, you worry. Is the cancer growing again? Could it be responsible for both the new skin irritations and today's feelings of crumminess and lethargy? Or do these flu-like symptoms have nothing to do with the cancer?

There is no way to know. You just have to wait and see.

I continue to read cancer blogs, soaking up information about treatments people have tried, drugs on the horizon, doctors that people like or don't like. It's stunning how many sad stories there are, and how many contradictory beliefs as to which therapies do or don't work. But I am good at ignoring the information that isn't relevant to our situation, discounting horror stories, and capturing details that might prove helpful later.

Lynn isn't able to do that. She started to look at some of the same websites and found herself stuck on the sad stories, the bad outcomes, the people whose treatments stopped working, and didn't know where to turn. When she mentioned some of these to Dr. Hellmann, he told her to stop reading the websites; they just mess with her head and make her fear outcomes she might never face. We both thought this was good advice.

Lynn and I start talking about fear, about pain, about death, and what comes after. It's not a topic we've ever discussed before.

Neither of us is religious. I was raised by a secular Jewish mother and a lapsed Episcopalian father. Their compromise was to avoid religion entirely. Our family never went to church, and Christmas was mainly an opportunity to hear beautiful music and exchange gifts under a highly decorated tree. When asked, I say I'm an atheist.

Lynn, too, was raised without religion. She doesn't believe in labels, refuses to call herself atheist or agnostic, but she doesn't go to church either.

"This would be a pretty good time to start believing in Heaven," she says one night. We are clearing the table, preparing to wash the dishes.

"That's a surprise. Are you really considering it?"

"I just thought it would be comforting to know what happens next."

"Less scary, perhaps?"

She shakes her head. "That's not it. Dying doesn't scare me. I imagine it's like falling into a really deep sleep. I'm much more afraid of pain."

"And after? Do you think your spirit will live on, without your body?"

"I don't know. No one does. That's the big mystery."

The idea of an unknowable mystery appeals to both of us. We don't think science has all the answers, but we don't believe religion does either. Rather than gaining strength from faith or a church community, we will have to find it within ourselves and in the support of family and friends.

～

Lynn may not be afraid of dying, but she is afraid of pain. She never again wants to experience the levels of pain she felt last fall, before the treatments kicked in.

So when some of the old sensations come back—an annoying tingling and irritation around her torso—we book an appointment with Dr. Yao, the neurosurgeon at Mt. Sinai. It doesn't matter that the Sloan Kettering radiologists can't see anything to worry about; we want a second opinion from someone we trust.

Dr. Yao spends almost half an hour with us, reviewing the latest MRI and addressing Lynn's symptoms. "I can't see anything in your spine that would explain the sensations," he says. "The tumors are shrinking nicely, and the bone is healing."

Dr. Yao calls the sensations "probably muscular," but I think that's what neurosurgeons always say when they can't identify the source of a pain. It's the same term everyone used last September, when Lynn went from doctor to doctor to figure out why her abdomen and back hurt so much while the tumors grew inside her. Hearing this phrase makes us anxious. Is something else starting to grow, something not visible on the scans? Should we be looking for it?

We share these thoughts on CaringBridge, but we don't let them color our public behavior. Our closest friends read the posts, so when they see us in person they don't need to ask about Lynn's cancer; they already know the latest, and we talk mostly of other things.

On the Saturday after Christmas, we host a family gathering in our small apartment, ostensibly a belated birthday party but really a celebration of life. Lynn spends two days cooking, and I make a big flan for dessert. We fill the room with our closest family, toasting each other around the table.

I'm especially pleased to see Francie's younger son, Peter. Last winter he withdrew from Cornell because of a heroin addiction, then spent the spring in rehab followed by a halfway house in California. He's only been back for a few weeks.

It's been a terrible year for Francie and Paul: researching addiction, finding treatment for their son, never knowing how it would turn out. Sort of like Lynn and me now.

Peter and Shirley at his sister's wedding

Peter was always a golden child, smart and creative in equal measure. It is wonderful to have him with us, full of life and talking about the semester to come. I think we all feel that way. Lynn and Peter have emerged from difficult places and are back in the sunlight.

After singing "Happy Birthday," I raise my glass and proudly toast, "To Lynn!" which embarrasses her. We don't explicitly toast Peter. His presence here is celebration enough.

Thursday, January 1, 2015
www.CaringBridge.org/LynnKotula

Last night we went to a great New Year's Eve party. Lynn danced for an hour and was still talking energetically with friends at 1:30 a.m., when I pooped out and we had to leave. Need I say more?

At the party, I had a long talk with a friend about the journey Lynn and I are on and the choices we've made. There are a lot of other routes she could have taken. For one, she could have stayed with Dr. Dar. He's a smart, caring doctor, and he's right in our neighborhood. Lynn would be on Tarceva right now and probably feeling just as good as she does today. Or she could be pursuing some of the more aggressive alternative therapies one learns about on the web, high doses of supplements and such, that Lynn is not allowed to take because of the rules of the clinical trial.

But through various twists and turns, we found our way to the team at Sloan Kettering, and she chose to place her trust in them. As a result, I can slow down my web research and Lynn doesn't need to read those sites. Dr.

Hellmann and his colleagues are reading the web pages and scientific studies for us; they know what other drugs and treatments are in the pipeline. They can help us navigate the side effects, and they are providing the MPDL3280A, which might make all the difference.

We made the choice quickly, like a shotgun marriage, but sometimes a shotgun marriage turns out to be a good thing.

Next Monday Lynn will have her first post-treatment CT scan, and on Wednesday she will learn the results. But as Dr. Hellmann reminded Lynn yesterday, what matters is that she feels much better. We don't need a scan to tell us that.

Tuesday, January 6, 2015

I'm walking down a corridor at work when Francie calls me on my cell phone.

"I have something to tell you," she says, her voice trembling. Then, after a long pause, "Peter's dead."

I lean against the wall for support and find myself sitting on the floor.

"When?" I manage to ask. "How?"

"Yesterday. It was an overdose."

She starts crying. Her grief is overwhelming; there is nothing I can say.

Later I will learn that Francie herself found the body when Peter didn't come down for dinner. I can't imagine anything worse.

Francie tells me they are planning the funeral for Saturday. Peter was very popular; it will be a big event.

Then she says, "I need you to tell Mom. I can't deal with that."

I don't know if I can deal with it either, but there is no one else.

We decide that I should wait until the last minute. I call Shirley and tell her that rather than having dinner tonight, as usual, I'd like to come over on Friday. She doesn't question this and says she looks forward to seeing me.

On Friday I wait until we are seated across from each other at her favorite restaurant. When I tell her that Peter has died she looks confused.

"Peter? Our Peter?"

"Yes."

"But we just saw him."

"I know, Mom. But it happened."

"How? Why?"

"He had a drug problem." This is something else we've never told her. "He used again, and it was too much for him."

For five minutes we cycle through the same few sentences. Shirley keeps saying "Peter?" in a stunned voice, and I keep saying "Yes," and telling her how it happened. Then a moment later, she says his name again. I don't know if it's because of cognitive decline or sheer shock, but her brain refuses to accept the news.

Eventually, I am able to move on and tell her that I will be back tomorrow morning to take her to the funeral, another disturbing idea that needs to be repeated four or five times.

Lynn and I wear purple to the funeral, Peter's favorite color, and afterwards we return to Francie's house for a buffet meal. Everything is happening so fast, it's impossible to believe he won't walk in the door any minute. When Francie snaps a photo of us, we hug each other tightly while smiling at the camera.

In the photo you can see that my arms wrap almost all the way around Lynn's body, pulling her to me. I am shaken and shattered by Peter's loss; it reminds me all too clearly that the people I love can be snatched away at any minute. For the time being, we still have each other, but how long will that last?

After Peter's funeral

Scanxiety

"We don't need a scan to tell us that it's working," I wrote on CaringBridge. But actually, we do.

No matter how often Dr. Hellmann says that what matters is how Lynn feels, the scans of her body—CTs of her lungs, MRIs of her spine, and full-body PET scans to see if the cancer has spread—are immensely important to us, providing concrete, measurable evidence of what is going on inside. To tell our friends otherwise is wishful thinking.

As we count down the days until we learn the results of the first scan, we become increasingly nervous, a feeling we soon learn is called "scanxiety." Are the tumors shrinking? By how much? And most tantalizingly, will the immunotherapy work a miracle and blow them away?

Full remission is almost unheard of in stage IV lung cancer patients, and both Dr. Dar and Dr. Hellmann have been careful not to promise any such thing. But on the web I read about patients for whom the new immunotherapy drugs perform exactly that miracle. Maybe Lynn will be one of the lucky ones.

Wednesday, January 7, 2015
www.CaringBridge.org/LynnKotula

I wish I could say "Wow" about Lynn's CT scan results, but actually they're just fine. Dr. Hellmann told us today that all of Lynn's tumors have shrunk, and there is evidence that her spinal bone is healing. If she were just on Tarceva, this would be good news indeed. But since she is also taking the immunotherapy, I had fantasized that the tumors would shrink much more—the word "dramatically" comes to mind. It's difficult to let it go.

We spent more than six hours today waiting for one thing or another. I passed the time reading articles about new drugs that are candidates to succeed Tarceva once it stops working. The early results are extremely promising. When the Tarceva stops, there's a good chance we'll be able to get another year (or perhaps several) of good quality life by taking one of these exciting drugs. It's all about buying time while hoping for a more permanent cure.

A few days later, Sloan sends a link to the radiology report, which unsettles us with details no one mentioned when we were there. While the main lung tumor has indeed shrunk, the secondary tumor remains unchanged, and now Lynn has a third, new nodule that is "suspicious for metastases."

This sounds scary. Where the heck did it come from? Also, the report says that Lynn's main spinal tumor is "sclerotic" and larger than before.

Although we are pretty sure this must not be bad news, or Dr. Hellmann would have told us last week, reading the report is unsettling. We call the team and speak with Maureen, who assures us that "sclerotic" is a good thing: It means the spinal tumor is dying and the surrounding bone is healing. She says the team thinks the new nodule in Lynn's lung is probably not a tumor but rather a "flare" in response to the immunotherapy, which should go away in time.

It will take a series of scans, over several months, to learn how Lynn's tumors respond to the drugs.

Wednesday, February 18, 2015
www.CaringBridge.org/LynnKotula

On Tuesday Lynn had her second CT scan since starting treatment, and on Wednesday we went to Sloan Kettering for the meeting with Dr. Hellmann.

Luckily, the results were "good" again, though the specifics were disappointing. Lynn's tumors are about the same size as six weeks ago. They are no longer growing, which is great, but they've also stopped shrinking. Rats! This is the sort of thing that happens with Tarceva on its own. I really wanted the MPDL to blow them away.

Dr. Hellmann would not be drawn into that kind of thinking. At times he seems like a cross between a therapist and Buddha, or perhaps Yoda. He speaks slowly and chooses his words carefully, and though he gives clear answers to direct questions, when Lynn tries to draw him out about bigger concerns, he turns them around with questions of his own. "Well, how do you feel? Do you feel good? Then that's good, isn't it?"

I think he's trying to get her to focus on what's really important, which is to enjoy life while the treatments are working. The future will come soon enough.

⌒

The writer and physician Oliver Sacks published a piece in the *New York Times* titled "My Own Life" about his response to learning he has incurable cancer. "I feel intensely alive," he wrote. "I feel a sudden clear focus and perspective... There is no time for anything inessential... I shall no longer look at *NewsHour* every night..."

This piece generates hundreds of comments, many of which praise Sacks for facing his disease and sharing his feelings so openly. But Lynn has a different response, which she describes in one of her rare CaringBridge posts.

Friday, February 20, 2015
www.CaringBridge.org/LynnKotula
by Lynn Kotula

Let me see if I can say this without sounding ungrateful. The Oliver Sacks piece pissed me off. I much prefer Susan Gubar, who writes the *Living with Cancer* blog at the *New York Times*. She allows for the whole range of emotions that many/most/all of us with severe and terminal illnesses (and their caregivers) might feel, and that includes so many less exalted feelings—cheated, pissed off, victimized, depressed, sad, terrified—and then, yes—happy: it's a wonderful day, I love that book, this movie, this painting, this person, this flavor, my cat.

Unlike Sacks I'm still interested in the news, and I hate to admit it, but I probably spend more time watching

Netflix than ever before—I look forward to it at the end of the day as something that I can (usually) count on to take me out of myself. You want to be able to waste your time, to do whatever you want.

I don't feel one bit brave, though I do look at all those people in the waiting rooms at Sloan Kettering, and my own dear friends who have faced their own illnesses or illnesses of their loved ones - and feel that they are the brave ones - even though in most cases I don't know how they feel at all.

I am surprised to see Lynn put her feelings front and center on CaringBridge and encouraged by the flood of supportive comments that she receives.

"Having been there, I know exactly what you mean about the 'less exalted feelings,'" writes our friend Jenny, a breast cancer survivor. "Boy, did I have a bunch of those—still do, sometimes. And three cheers for Netflix, the best escape ever!"

And Carmela, an artist who has undergone multiple heart surgeries because of Marfan syndrome, writes:

When I got sick (the third time), I bought the biggest damn TV I could find and subscribed to every TV service I like. In fact, I now have three big TVs for different rooms in the house. I buy the *National Enquirer* and never care who sees it on my coffee table. I buy myself little gifts online all the time. Just when I'm feeling blue, John will announce "Package for Carmela!" I can only paint an hour or two a day, if that, but I believe this attitude has helped my work as well. I'm not as worried about what others think. I know what pleases me. I don't know

> whether this means anything to you, or not. I just wanted
> to share my experience on getting through day-to-day
> life with a chronic illness.

About a week later, we log into Sloan's online portal and
see that the latest radiology report is now available. It says
things like: "Peribronchial right upper lobe mass measures 2.3 x 1.2 cm previously 2.1 x 1.3 cm . . . Right lower
lobe nodule measures 1.2 x 1.2 cm previously 1.2 x .09
cm . . . New peripheral clustered nodules in the right lower
lobe measuring up to 0.5 cm, possibly infectious inflam-
matory . . . ."

This doesn't completely freak us out, but it is scary. We
need a better explanation. What do Lynn's doctors think
when they read this stuff? Why is this "good?"

We decide that I will accompany Lynn to her next
appointment so we can hear the answers together.

Wednesday, March 11, 2015

Dr. Jamie Chaft is covering for Dr. Hellmann while he's
on duty at the hospital. Dr. Chaft is a small woman who
wears tall boots and moves with quick energy, quite different from Dr. Hellmann's studied calm. We met her
once before, but on that visit we didn't click and thought
she was in a bit of a hurry—smart but cool.

Today we like her a lot. Almost the first thing she says,
offhandedly while she walks past us to a chair, is: "The
most important thing is that this isn't a lot of cancer;
the tumors are really small, and they're in insignificant
locations."

What... ? You could have knocked me over with a feather. Lynn's cancer is deadly if left untreated, but no one told us we were starting in such a good position.

Next comes Dr. Chaft's version of what Dr. Hellmann always emphasizes: confirming that Lynn is feeling good, leading a full life, and experiencing relatively minor side effects. "This is what we want most," she says. "The fact that the drugs are holding back a stage IV cancer without life-impairing side effects is a major achievement."

Then she discusses the margin of error in the CT scans, which take 1 mm "slices" of images. "With tumors as small as yours, the minor changes in size of 1 or 2 mm from one scan to the next are not significant and might not even be real."

In this regard, only one of Lynn's tumors is potentially dangerous: The one in her right lower lobe that appeared after treatment began, which grew slightly from the first scan to the second.

"We don't know about that nodule," admits Dr. Chaft. "It might be a flare, or it might be a real tumor that is biologically different from the others and therefore not responding to the drugs. Or it might be something else."

From the team's perspective, it is quite small, slow growing, and not causing Lynn any distress. They will watch it closely but don't feel any urgency.

This pattern will continue for the next five years. Lynn's tumors will slowly grow and shrink, as if pulsing or breathing on a very long time scale. But they will never get a lot smaller, and they won't, during those years, grow much bigger. After a few more scans, we stop thinking about them. We learn how to decipher the radiology reports and no longer feel that I need to accompany Lynn every time.

It takes us much longer to internalize how good this is. Despite how often Dr. Hellmann says that Lynn is in a good place, and how often I write in CaringBridge that "stability is good," it doesn't sink in until later that summer, when we watch an episode of the monthly *Lung Cancer Living Room*® webcast in which an oncologist says that his patients are often disappointed when he tells them their disease is stable. They don't understand the value of the word.

"For someone with late-stage cancer, stable disease is a home run!" he says. "Cancer wants to grow, and each month you keep it from growing you are winning. If you can shrink it, that's great, like pitching a no-hitter, but it doesn't change the outcome: stable means winning."

Hearing these words from a stranger works better than when we heard the same message from Lynn's oncologists. For the first time, we realize that she is similar to those patients who hope for full remission and are disappointed at anything less. Lynn's tumors are stable! That's great news. We just have to learn how to make the most of each day and deal with the side effects.

⌒

By March, both of us are starting to feel confident. We've survived the whirlwind and come out the other side— stumbling, still finding our footing, but with the sense that we are entering a good period.

Lynn has an infusion every three weeks, but I no longer take time off to accompany her. A rotation of friends volunteers to meet her in the outpatient pavilion, where they chat cheerfully as the experimental drug drips into her vein.

Lynn is also, finally, able to start painting again in her repaired studio. Before long she is spending hours at a time there, standing quietly at her easel with music playing, working on one painting after another.

Now that she feels her time is limited, she wants to make as many paintings as she can. Instead of spending hours setting up a scene, she puts a few objects on the table and starts painting them almost immediately, less thinking, more doing. The paintings—generally smaller than her previous ones and less carefully arranged—come more easily to her and seem more alive. Critics and other artists respond as well, telling her she is doing some of her best work. It is a surprising gift from her cancer.

Friday, March 13, 2015
www.CaringBridge.org/LynnKotula

These past few weeks have felt like a dream—a dream almost without cancer. Don't pinch me, I don't want to wake up.

Lynn says that in her version of the dream, cancer is very much present, mostly in the things she cannot eat: no coffee, no salads, no roughage, no nuts or seeds, no beans, no dark-green vegetables. And in the fact that we cannot plan a vacation because how could we take long walks with no easy access to bathrooms, and what would Lynn eat? And the daily consideration of how many Loperamides to take to ward off diarrhea, and the need to limit meals out with friends to ensure she will make it home without an accident, not to mention the odd stomach rumblings after eating certain foods. But compared to where we were just a few months ago, this is a beautiful dream.

Lynn and I assume we'll have at least six months, perhaps two or three years, before things go wrong again. It doesn't occur to us that we'll only have two weeks.

COLLATERAL DAMAGE

Sunday, March 29, 2015

It's another sunny Sunday afternoon. We are hurrying down Broadway toward the 96th Street express stop, heading to a play in Brooklyn, when Lynn gasps and stops short.

"Something's wrong," she says, looking puzzled and a little afraid.

She catches her breath and tries to continue walking, but after a few steps she stops again. "I can't do this."

There's a new pain in the middle of her spine, sharp and hot, near where they zapped the tumor. With every step, it sends an electric shock through her torso. She has to go home and lie down.

Lynn encourages me to continue on by myself; perhaps this will pass, whatever it is. I flag a cab for her and then take the subway to the theater. The play is terrific—it will go on to win several awards—but I have a hard time enjoying it and can't wait to get home.

That evening we call Sloan Kettering for advice on which painkillers to take, but when Lynn describes her symptoms, the nurse transfers us to an on-call doctor who tells her to come in immediately. We're a little freaked out, but at least we don't have to sit home worrying. I help Lynn downstairs and into a taxi.

We spend four hours in Sloan's Urgent Care Unit, which is like an emergency room for Sloan Kettering patients. A doctor gives Lynn a standard neurological exam, testing the strength and sensation in her limbs, balance, motor control, etc. All are fine. There's no indication her spinal cord is compromised, which is what they most fear. But they don't know what is causing the pain.

They send us home with a prescription for Percocet and arrange for Lynn to have a spinal MRI the next day. I scramble to rearrange my work schedule to accompany her to the MRI, since traveling has suddenly become much more difficult.

The scan is on Monday, but we have to wait another day for a radiologist to review it and write the report. Now we're enduring a new kind of scanxiety, focused on Lynn's spine rather than her lungs.

Dr. Hellmann calls on Tuesday with the results. They can see an "infraction" in the area where her spinal tumor was zapped.

"What does that mean?" asks Lynn.

"It's a minor crushing of the bone," says Dr. Hellmann. "Basically, a small piece of your spine is crumbling."

There is also some swelling, so Dr. Hellmann prescribes a quick flood of steroids to see if they reduce the pain. They won't solve the underlying problem but should help Lynn get out of bed while the doctors figure out what to do next.

The steroids help but not enough. Lynn is in terrible pain and barely leaves the house, so Dr. Hellmann refers us to Dr. George Krol, a neuroradiologist who specializes in spinal interventions. Dr. Hellmann says he particularly likes Dr. Krol because he is very conservative and will not recommend surgery unless there is no better option.

The good news: Percocet causes constipation, so once Lynn starts taking it for back pain, her diarrhea disappears.

Sunday, April 5, 2015
www.CaringBridge.org/LynnKotula

This morning we found ourselves in an emotional conversation like the ones we had last fall. When the pain struck early in the week and new nodules appeared on Lynn's CT scan, the doctors initially couldn't figure out what was wrong. It was extremely frightening, as if a hand had come through the window and snatched her life away. She was stuck at home, wondering how long this will go on, and whether it is the start of a long downward slide.

All this provides another example of how cancer can radically change your perspective. I've always been skeptical about back surgery; it can sometimes do more harm than good, and I've read that placebos (including placebo surgery) can be as effective for back pain as drugs or surgery. But now Lynn has significant pain where we can see what appears to be the cause. It's not a mystery. And Sloan Kettering has world-class neurosurgeons who specialize in dealing with complications of spinal metastases. If the pain remains constant and the treatment team says, "We know how to deal with this," I would be inclined to follow their lead and do whatever they suggest.

Tuesday, April 7, 2015

Unlike virtually every other doctor we've seen at Sloan Kettering, Dr. Krol is closer to seventy than thirty, with thick white hair and a strong Polish accent. Both he and his nurse, Abby, spend a lot of time with us, reviewing Lynn's symptoms and the MRI.

On the screen we can see the fractured vertebra in the middle of Lynn's back, just below where her tumor was zapped. "We know how to fix this," says Dr. Kroll. "There's a procedure called a Balloon Kyphoplasty that is very good for this kind of fracture."

But he doesn't want to do the procedure now. "The fracture is smaller than I would expect, given your high level of pain. I think most of what you're feeling may be muscle spasms. If we can eliminate the spasms, perhaps the fracture will heal on its own." He refers us to another doctor, Martin Chen, an anesthesiologist in Sloan Kettering's Pain Management group.

When we see Dr. Chen, two days later, he examines Lynn closely and locates a large, tightly-clenched muscle exactly where Lynn says her back hurts most. He proposes to inject it with a variant of Novocaine.

Lynn flinches, saying she doesn't want it; she's afraid the needle will hurt more than it helps. But Dr. Chen assures her that after the first jab, she will hardly feel a thing. Reluctantly, Lynn bends over the table while he fills a large syringe to which he attaches a scarily long needle.

He then spends several minutes circling Lynn, making multiple injections into the swollen muscle. Within minutes, it shrinks to its normal size.

After Lynn puts on her shirt, she is able to walk all the way to Madison Avenue and take the bus home, which feels like a miracle given the past two weeks.

The injection succeeds in reducing Lynn's muscle spasms, but there is still a constant core pain emanating from the fractured vertebra. Lynn doesn't want to take more Percocet because it gives her painful constipation and bad episodes of lightheadedness. For the next five days, she doesn't leave the house.

Several times I suggest we try the kyphoplasty, but the idea scares her too much. She is deeply afraid of doing something that could make her back worse.

Lynn's daily pattern: sleeps poorly at night, wakes every hour, gets up feeling mildly miserable. Cries at least once, takes Percocet, goes back to bed. Sleeps soundly for several good hours (sometimes both morning and afternoon). Feels both physically and emotionally better after naps. Talks at length with friends on the phone, pets the cat, cooks often. In the evening, we watch at least one episode of *Breaking Bad* together, followed by an episode of *Mad Men* to calm us down. Then read a little in bed, turn out the light, start over.

Some of our friends have extensive experience with long-term pain, and they fill CaringBridge with suggestions for getting through the day. But it's hard to avoid the elephant in the room. Spending your days indoors, unable to do most of the things that give meaning to your life, is deeply depressing. That's true for Lynn, but it also affects me as her caregiver and partner. We're stuck here together, waiting for something to break the pattern.

When we get down to one last episode of *Mad Men*, Lynn agrees that we'd better do something before we run out of shows to watch. She calls Dr. Krol and schedules the kyphoplasty.

Thursday, April 16, 2015

We spend the day at Sloan where Lynn undergoes the Balloon Kyphoplasty procedure. We had expected it to be performed by Dr. Krol, but he had to fly to Seattle for his grandson's First Communion, so he introduces us to his colleague Dr. Lis.

Dr. Lis is enthusiastic. When I call him "boyish," Lynn calls him "goofy." Apparently he and Dr. Krol, both of Polish heritage, have their own little corner of Sloan Kettering, a department of two.

Once Lynn is fully sedated, Dr. Lis inserts two needles into her collapsed vertebra, through which he inflates a balloon to create a space where the vertebra ought to be. Then he injects a kind of "cement" into that space and allows it to harden, restoring the vertebra to its original contour and also strengthening the area.

It all sounded rather miraculous when Dr. Krol explained it, but in the recovery room Lynn feels terrible, sparking a commotion among the nurses and doctors that suggests her response is worse than usual. Dr. Lis had to push aside some ribs to get to the vertebra, leaving a bruise-like pain. In addition, Lynn experiences complications from being intubated while lying on her stomach and feels as if she can't breathe. When I see her, she is wearing a nebulizer and is visibly shaking. Her face is red and teary.

Over the next ninety minutes, assisted by a welcome shot of Dilaudid, most of her discomfort fades. Eventually, Lynn feels good enough to walk out of the hospital unassisted, and on the street she tells me that she is now able to twist her torso to the right for the first time in several weeks. It's hard to know how much of that represents real spinal recovery and how much is the Dilaudid.

From the doctor's perspective, everything went well. We know this because, while we are waiting for the elevator, Dr. Lis comes bounding down the hallway, catching us as the doors open. What he wants to say, with all his enthusiasm, is not only how well the procedure went, but that it quickly became clear Lynn needed it.

"Her T12 vertebra was surprisingly soft—porous— probably a result of the intensive radiation. If we hadn't done the kyphoplasty, it would have continued to collapse, causing even more pain. It never would have healed on its own."

When I post about this on CaringBridge, our friend Carmela helps us put it in perspective. "I had two ribs removed to enable surgeons to work on my descending aorta," she writes. "Knowing that movie stars (like Cher) have had their ribs removed cosmetically, I asked my surgeon if he could improve my figure too? He just laughed."

"Hi Carmela," replies Lynn, "I can't begin to imagine what you've been through. My complaints put me to shame when I think of what you and John, Flavia, Jenny, Nancy, Libby—so many friends and their families—have been through. Oh, dear Life!! And how wonderful when we're able to win a bit or all of it back for a time."

Sunday, April 19, 2015
www.CaringBridge.org/LynnKotula

Although the kyphoplasty was a success and the majority of Lynn's back pain is gone, we didn't anticipate how many levels of crappiness would follow. There is substantial new pain caused by the intrusion of those two needles, plus lingering irritations caused by the face-down intubation. A war is raging in Lynn's intestines as her system changes from Percocet-driven constipation to good old Tarceva-driven diarrhea, leaving her extremely tired: a weary, internally-driven fatigue that does not correlate to physical activity. She's back to staying home and spending a lot of time in bed.

Lynn finds this all quite depressing, and so do I. We had to miss our friend Laura's birthday and dance party, which we had anticipated for weeks.

Instead, we cuddled on the couch and watched *Life Itself*, a terrific biography of Roger Ebert, though it focused extensively on the last six months of his life when he was dealing with cancer. Watching this, we couldn't help but compare ourselves to Ebert and his caregivers, wondering how much we will have to face down the road, and how well we will handle it if seriously bad things happen.

Lynn's studio is a twenty-minute walk from our apartment, and once there, she has to climb ninety steps to get to the top floor. She manages the journey two or three times but then stops going, leaving a half-finished painting on the easel.

Dr. Hellmann orders several tests, but none of them reveal anything. Once again, we are in limbo, waiting and hoping for something to change.

Friday, April 24, 2015
www.CaringBridge.org/LynnKotula

A lot can happen when you're being treated for cancer. About a week ago, Lynn had a conversation with a long-term cancer patient whom she met in her support group at Mount Sinai. Barbara is living with two incurable cancers and has had many invasive treatments over the past six years. She told Lynn that this is how the process works: You live for a while in a kind of equilibrium (as we did from December through March), and then something happens that rocks your world; they figure out what it is and treat it; and then (hopefully) you find a new equilibrium and start over. Right now, our world is still rocking.

It already occurred to us that the fracture in Lynn's spine is probably collateral damage from the radiation. Now Dr. Krol's nurse says that a successful kyphoplasty can itself cause collateral damage by putting pressure on the vertebrae immediately above or below the treated one. There is no such thing as a free lunch.

Lynn takes a Percocet whenever she experiences serious pain, sometimes several times a day, so she asks Dr. Hellmann whether it would be okay to drink alcohol with her Percocet.

"If it makes you feel good, why not?" he says. Behind him, Maureen's eyes widen in surprise.

Lynn asks them if it would be okay to start swimming again or ride a bike, and Dr. Hellmann says, "Sure, anything that makes you feel good."

But the next day, Dr. Sebi Varghese, Lynn's new physical therapist, says "Absolutely not!" No swimming, no bike riding, no lifting even of milk containers until Sebi can adjust Lynn's posture and relieve the pressure on her spine, a process that will take many more sessions.

Lynn now spends a lot of time going to doctor's appointments and therapy sessions. They are a huge part of our lives, and there is rarely a day when she can stand in her studio and paint. Or at least, it feels that way.

"How are you doing?" asks Dr. Hellmann, each time we see him.

"Pretty good. A little sore, but overall it's been a good week."

I shake my head and interrupt. "That's not quite right. Just yesterday, you had a hard time getting out of bed. You said your ribs hurt again. And on Monday, you had to take several extra pain meds."

Lynn whacks my leg. "Shut up! It's my story, you don't know what I feel. Let me decide what's important."

For several visits I try, and fail, to give Dr. Hellmann a fuller picture, until I finally accept that I need to stop doing this. Hopefully, he realizes by now that Lynn will not share the full extent of her pain.

The upside of all these appointments is that we're starting to get the hang of Sloan Kettering. We have a better sense of what to expect and what the jargon means.

But we also feel like we're trapped on a hamster wheel, and Lynn is increasingly aware that everything she has is fragile. It's hard to make plans more than a day in advance when you don't know how you'll feel tomorrow, or what you'll be able to do next week. Most of us don't spend time thinking this way; we live in willful denial. Having cancer makes that denial difficult to achieve.

In many of these posts, I have downplayed painful details and barely mentioned our periods of depression. I was afraid that if the posts were too dark, our friends would abandon us. But now, for the first time, I share some of our gloom.

Saturday, May 9, 2015
www.CaringBridge.org/LynnKotula

It's starting to feel like a slog: an endless trudge through a muddy landscape. The cancer is incurable, the treatment process can never stop. So when we have setbacks, they weigh on us doubly. Damn, we're going in the wrong direction. Will this never end? No, it won't.

Last Monday I came home from work to find Lynn in bed again because of pain and fatigue. It was a new pain, more sore than sharp, higher up her back and not necessarily centered on her spine. We speculated that it was probably muscular, probably caused by the kyphoplasty, probably just a blip that will eventually go away.

Each morning we talked about Lynn's pain in minute detail, a mapping exercise that is guaranteed to frustrate because it's impossible to locate and quantify an experience as ephemeral as pain. Is it stronger than yesterday? In the same spot? Maybe yes, maybe no. It's hard for Lynn to describe exactly what she's feeling, hard to remember exactly what yesterday's pain felt like.

As the week progressed, it became clear that this new pain is not receding and may be intensifying. When we run our fingers down her spine, we think we can feel the exact vertebra into which Dr. Lis injected the cement. It is bigger than the ones above and below it, with a smoother, fuller surface. Perhaps it is *too* big now. Is there anything to be done about that?

We still do things together; we still laugh, and we know it is possible this week's pain will pass. But for me, this journal is about our journey (they are the same word, after all). The emotional impact of this week—the unexpected setback, the shift into "slog" mode, the realization that this may happen again and again—is a significant milestone, and I want to capture it. Not every journal entry needs to have a happy ending or a clear path forward.

I am nervous when I click the Publish button, but our friends lean in with much-needed support.

11 Comments

Thank you for your honesty. I want to go on this journey with you. —Orin

It means a lot to me to know what is happening. Staying in touch isn't just the good news. —Marion

∽

We start to look ahead to Blairstown, the rural New Jersey town where, for almost thirty summers, we have rented a sparsely furnished apartment from the painter Lois Dodd.

The house is a large white Victorian with clapboard walls that connect at interesting angles, leaded glass windows, and a gabled slate roof. Lois paints there during the winter but goes to Maine in the summer, leaving the second floor to us.

In Blairstown, we are immersed in art and nature: the walls and closets are filled with paintings, Lois's studio is just down the hall, and there is a large deck that opens out from the living room where we eat our meals, surrounded by trees. Five miles down the road is a national park where we hike, swim in beautiful lakes, and ride our bikes on country roads.

Furniture isn't important to Lois. There are a few comfortable chairs but no beds—she, and we, sleep on mattresses on the floor. Moving out there, carrying our luggage and supplies up the stairs, settling in, sleeping on the floor, driving back and forth each weekend, all loom like major challenges. Can we really do this?

Lynn begins researching beds and mattresses, while I wait and hope her pain will recede on its own. All this cancer-related planning is exhausting; I crave a few weeks just to live life without thinking about it.

In early June, Lynn feels a new pain, sharp and focused, in the middle of her spine, as if another vertebra has fractured. Because it keeps appearing and then fading, and because we really want to believe that it will heal on its own, we hold off telling Lynn's doctors for another week. Once we do, Dr. Krol immediately orders a spinal MRI.

This is Lynn's fifth spinal MRI since late September, which equals the number of lung scans she's had. This metric says a lot about Lynn's experience of her cancer.

If only it had metastasized to, say, a toenail instead of her spine, things might've been a lot easier.

Tuesday, June 16, 2015

Dr. Krol calls us with the results: Two more vertebrae are fractured, T11 and T9, where Lynn's tumor was radiated.

When we meet with Dr. Krol, he doesn't push her. He carefully shows the before and after images of Lynn's spine, so she can see the fractures in what had previously been intact bone. We discuss possible causes, including the radiation, pressure caused by the kyphoplasty, and Lynn's cancer. We will never know which of these is most responsible.

Dr. Krol raises the possibility of not doing anything and letting the vertebrae heal on their own. This appeals greatly to Lynn, since her experiences during and after her kyphoplasty were so painful. But then he says, "The fractures might heal, but it is more likely they won't, and they could even collapse further and endanger your spinal cord. If you're going to do a kyphoplasty, now is the time."

We sit in silence for a long moment. From my perspective, it's a no-brainer, but I'm not the one experiencing the pain. I bite my tongue and hold still.

Then Lynn nods and says, "Yes, let's do it."

A week later, in a multi-hour procedure, she undergoes three more kyphoplasties because a third vertebra has also collapsed.

～

It takes ten days for the fallout from the procedure to fade. There is back pain, an upset stomach, and nausea, as well as days when Lynn feels good in the morning and then exhausted and miserable in the afternoon, leading her to fear she may never feel healthy again.

Then on July 3, Lynn has a lovely, pain-free day as we drive out to Blairstown for the holiday, where suddenly the world seems full of promise. For the first time in several years, we see woodpeckers eating ripe cherries in the tree beside our deck, and then we go to a July 4th pig roast where we dance to Motown tunes. All day Lynn has been nervous about whether she will enjoy the party, but she has a great time, swirling to the music and kicking up her heels.

Sunday, July 12, 2015
www.CaringBridge.org/LynnKotula

Lynn and I have been talking about "coming to terms" with the permanency of her situation. Each time she has a good day, we say, "Oh, you're getting better" and we're excited, but then the next morning she wakes up in pain, and we're disappointed, sometimes even depressed.

We both want to believe that as long as she follows doctor's orders and does everything right, she will eventually be fine. But it doesn't work that way. Lynn's not fine, and she's not going to be fine, ever. By fine, I mean the person whose body was the source of so much pleasure, a body that helped her paint and swim and walk forever. This intimate and essential part of her is exactly what she has lost.

She now realizes that even as she tries hard to be a good girl and do everything she's supposed to do—taking her Tarceva every day like clockwork, going to all her appointments, keeping a record of every pill she swallows—she secretly expects at the end of each cycle that she'll finally be "better," when all she's really achieved is the completion of another bottle of pills.

When Lynn first told our friend Keith about the impact cancer has had on her life, he said, "Well, we're all heading that way, you just got there ahead of us." He meant living, aging, the journey we all share.

Last night Keith was at a party with us, and as we were leaving Lynn apologized that she hadn't had a chance to talk with him. "Don't worry," he said, "it was great seeing you here. You look beautiful tonight, and that's all I need to know."

You Can Do This

By late summer I am exhausted, the bone-deep fatigue young parents feel, though I'm almost sixty years old and there are no children in sight. When Lynn has setbacks or needs to make a decision, I am right there with her, going to appointments, holding her hand, planning next steps. It is all-consuming. At the same time, I'm trying to keep up with the demands of a full-time job, while also visiting my friend Sue every Monday and my mother every Tuesday, with whom I have to watch my words, so I don't reveal too much.

"You can do this," I keep telling myself. "You can do this."

As the months pass, I become physically and mentally drained and increasingly distracted. In July, I take our car in for its annual inspection. After I bring it back, I notice steam rising from under the hood. Without thinking, I open the hood and remove the plastic cap from the water reservoir to check the level. The water pump has broken and the reservoir is full of steam, which erupts like a geyser, seriously scalding my hand.

I spend the rest of the day with doctors, first at urgent care and then with a plastic surgeon. For the next month, I slather my hand with ointments and make weekly visits to the plastic surgeon to see whether I will need skin grafts. Luckily, the skin heals, but this is yet another drain on my time, as I am now taking care of myself while also trying to support Lynn.

Then three weeks later, while on vacation in Blairstown, Lynn feels pain and weakness in her legs, and I have another, more serious, accident.

Friday, August 21, 2015
www.CaringBridge.org/LynnKotula

Because of Lynn's condition, we haven't been able to do much walking together, so I've been taking ninety-minute bicycle rides in one direction or another. On Wednesday, the sky looked placid, but I got caught in a torrential thunderstorm. I continued riding for the next few miles, steadily uphill and reasonably safe. The rain eased as I neared the top, so when I started down the other side, I thought the worst was behind me.

Unfortunately, after a short distance, there was a slightly steeper downhill stretch, which ends where the road crosses a bridge over I-80. There is a bump and a pavement change as you go onto the bridge. I had been pumping the bike's brakes to keep them dry, but when I picked up speed, the brakes were useless. I hit the bump at thirty miles an hour, lost control, and slid sideways across the bridge until I slammed into the curb.

Luckily, my helmet protected my head and absorbed the impact, leaving my neck unaffected. But I broke three ribs behind my right lung and sustained significant road rash. In severe pain, all I could do was lie there as the rain poured down.

Several drivers stopped, called EMS, and I was taken by ambulance to the local hospital. A CT scan showed some internal bleeding, which meant I was at risk for complications, so they transferred me to the nearest trauma center, thirty miles away, where I spent the next thirty-six hours under observation.

I was discharged yesterday afternoon and am now with Lynn in Blairstown, but I'm in constant pain, which is controlled by OxyContin and an occasional Percocet. I can't drive or carry anything heavy. They told me I shouldn't go back to work for at least a week, and it will take six or eight weeks to completely heal.

What makes this even more ironic, if that's the word, is that three weeks ago I got a second-degree burn on the back of my left hand, which basically immobilized it for a week; then our kitchen sink here in Blairstown was clogged, and the plumber was unavailable because he had just totaled his truck; and when our friend St. Clair drove me back from Morristown Hospital yesterday, we were rear-ended by a young woman who was talking on her cellphone!

I like to end on a positive note, but the only thing I can think of is that our cat, Jack, who howled all night after Lynn returned from visiting me, thus scaring her because we think he, too, is on borrowed time, has recovered and is doing just fine.

20 Comments

Jeez, bring on the locusts, bring on the boils! You have to either laugh 'til you cry or vice versa. Certainly more eventful than any vacation I've had. —Libby

What I don't mention is that before the accident, when the thunderstorm blew in and the sky turned black and the wind buffeted me every which way, it didn't occur to me to stop cycling and find shelter. I hunched over the handlebars and pumped the pedals, saying to myself: You can do this. You can do this.

Later I realized that this is what I'd been telling myself for the past ten months.

I think these two accidents, the crash and the burn, were my body's way of saying, "No, you can't." And if I couldn't see that for myself, my body would find a way to tell me.

The timing of my accident couldn't be worse. When Lynn returns to Blairstown after visiting me in the hospital, she has so much pain in her legs that she has to crawl up the stairs on her hands and knees. The severe pain continues throughout the night. Now we are both in pain and unable to support each other.

Lynn is afraid to drive, so the next day a friend brings her to visit me at the trauma center. When she describes the deterioration in her symptoms, I bully her into calling Sloan Kettering, which she'd been reluctant to do. Dr. Hellmann tells her she needs an MRI right away and suggests she go immediately to the ER or an urgent care center.

Sitting in Morristown Hospital, we explain the situation to my nurse, who calls an aide to wheel Lynn down to the ER. A work colleague, who came to visit me, ends up spending almost eight hours with Lynn, and then drives her back to Blairstown at midnight.

The next day the Morristown radiologist calls to say that even though there is no spinal compression, he can see something abnormal at the base of Lynn's spine, but he's unable to tell whether this new abnormality is a "fracture in place" or a new tumor. It's one more thing we will need to figure out when we are strong enough to drive back to New York.

Two days later we are in the kitchen in Blairstown while Lynn prepares dinner. We are both on strong pain medications, which disorient us and heighten our emotions.

When Lynn crouches down to get something from the fridge, she hears a weird popping sound and feels a sudden stab in her lower back. I rush over and help her to a chair, where she starts hyperventilating to control the pain. It's impossible even to consider spending another night in Blairstown.

Luckily, our friends downstairs are willing to drive us into the city. We leave behind an unmade bed, dirty dishes, and a half-drunk glass of milk, like a family evacuating before a hurricane.

We arrive at Sloan's Urgent Care Center a little after midnight, where Lynn is seen by the entire on-site neurology team. They do a thorough workup to learn the extent of her limitations, and, most importantly, try to determine whether her problem is pain or weakness, which would indicate a neurological problem.

Lynn is unable to walk much and is in danger of falling when she does. Based on her symptoms and the MRI report from Morristown, the attending physician decides that she probably has a small hip fracture. At about 9:00 a.m., she is admitted as a thoracic oncology patient, and the doctors spend the next thirty-six hours trying to figure out what is going on in her body.

Despite the uncertainty, Lynn is in good spirits.

"Isn't this nuts?" she writes on CaringBridge. "This building has a really motley and sometimes wonderful assortment of art work on the walls. When they wheeled me down the corridor, I saw some early paintings by my teacher Paul Resika sailing by."

While in the hospital, we get to see how the teams we've been dealing with work together.

As an outpatient, Lynn had to call each department directly, and the collaboration occurred somewhere behind the scenes. In the hospital, the doctors come to you, sometimes together. We can see how well the teams communicate with each other because each team member seems up-to-date with whatever we discussed with their predecessors. And we're particularly lucky because our friend Dr. Chaft, who happens to be on call this week, is in charge of Lynn's care.

Friday, August 28, 2015
www.CaringBridge.org/LynnKotula

In every conversation, the goal was to restore Lynn's quality of life. It wasn't a question of which procedure will "cure" her or how best to fix the fracture. The question was, how can we get Lynn back on her feet and able to enjoy life again?

The people we interacted with—doctors, nurses, aides, and technicians— seemed happy to be there. Several told us they much prefer Sloan Kettering to other hospitals where they've worked. One spent half an hour describing how Sloan supported her through night school as she worked her way up from an assistant answering phones to a full-fledged nurse, all while raising three kids. Even the cafeteria is top-notch. Whenever you're hungry, you order from an à la carte menu that includes Maryland Crab Cakes and Asian Sea Bass, and then they bring it to you within an hour—and it's really good!

It doesn't hurt that Sloan has so much money. We asked a doctor how they could possibly afford to pay for all the services Lynn received. "Rich people," he said, "who either make major donations to get their names on the buildings or fly from around the world and pay the full price for their treatment." Patients like Lynn benefit from this de facto income redistribution. It's not a scalable model, and it's a terrible way to distribute great health care around the country, but it's available to anyone, rich or poor, who comes to Sloan.

On Tuesday the doctors decide that Lynn has a sacral insufficiency fracture, a hairline crack in the large triangular bone at the base of her spine, and Dr. Chaft sends us home.

There is little one can do to treat such a fracture; the most conservative course is to take pain medication while it heals on its own. For three days, Lynn wears a low-dose fentanyl patch that sends a steady stream of opiates into her system, and she takes a Percocet when the pain is more than the fentanyl can handle. Unfortunately, this is pretty much all the time. She signs up for at-home physical therapy, but when the therapist arrives Lynn is in too much pain to have a session.

Lynn could keep increasing the fentanyl, but she hates the wooziness that comes with it, so after a few days she has me peel off the patch and makes an appointment to receive a nerve-blocking injection.

The entire week is exhausting and utterly depressing. We don't sleep while in the hospital, and our pain prevents us from having uninterrupted sleep once we're home. Worse, the fracture appeared out of the blue without a triggering event. What is to prevent more fractures in the future? Intellectually, we have answers: pain management, physical therapy, bone strengthening drugs, possibly another operation. But emotionally, it is exceptionally hard, and there are no promises as to what the future will bring.

Sunday, August 30, 2015
www.CaringBridge.org/LynnKotula

We went to the pain management appointment with high hopes, expecting Lynn to receive a nerve block injection into her sacrum. Instead, Dr. Chen injected an anesthetic into the muscles on Lynn's left side because that's where she had more pain. We were there for several hours and came away confused and disappointed, and Lynn was in tears after the procedure because Dr. Chen left her alone to get dressed and find her way back to the waiting room. He may be a technical genius, but he seemed blind to Lynn's emotional fragility.

It is now more than a year since Lynn started trying to figure out what was wrong with her, and almost ten months since she began cancer treatment. During this year she's had about three months of feeling good. The rest have been weighted with one type of pain or another.

Tomorrow we have to decide who to call.

Looking back at this post, I find what I omitted more interesting than what I wrote.

On Friday evening, we came home from the pain management appointment exhausted and dispirited. We walked straight to the bedroom and collapsed on the bed together, still wearing our coats. I started sobbing, saying, "I can't do this," over and over while Lynn stroked my arm.

For the first time, I told her how hard the year had been for me. "I feel like I've been pulling you from one treatment to another," I sobbed, "and so many times you didn't want them, and I had to talk you into them. It's hard, so hard. I can't keep doing this. I just don't have the strength."

All year long I'd kept these feelings to myself. Lynn told me several times that she was afraid her cancer, and all the effort it took to care for her, would drive me away. So when I had difficult thoughts—that maybe it would be better if Lynn died sooner rather than later, or that I really missed being able to have sex the way we used to—the last thing I could do was share them with her. I wanted her to have total faith that I would be by her side, no matter what it took.

Now, sobbing and shaking, I was having some kind of breakdown, and it was clear that I couldn't go on like that. I had to let her know how I really felt, even if doing so risked pushing her away.

Gently Lynn wrapped her arms around me and pulled me to her. She touched her forehead to mine and stroked my hair, saying, "I understand, really I do, it makes perfect sense," over and over, until my breathing eased and I slowly stopped shaking.

Fifteen years earlier, on our first trip to Vietnam, Lynn and I took a long walk through the back streets of Hanoi. After about an hour of twists and turns, we came to a large boulevard that separated us from our hotel.

"How are we going to cross?" asked Lynn.

Five lanes of traffic passed ceaselessly before us, a river of bicycles, motorbikes, and a few lonely autos all racing in the same direction. The nearest traffic lights were so far away they could barely be seen, and the traffic never stopped.

"I have no idea," I said.

We were about to give up and walk to the distant corner when a movement caught my eye. Fifty feet to our left, an elderly man dressed in black stepped off the curb. Lynn gasped, I held my breath, but somehow nothing hit him. He walked steadily across the stream of traffic, as if through flowing water. Then he was on the far side and disappeared into the distance.

Had we imagined it?

A minute later a young woman stepped into the traffic. Lynn shook her head and said, "I can't do that, it scares me too much."

"Wait," I said. "I think I'm getting this."

The third time someone crossed the street, I realized how they did it.

"Look," I said. "They wait until there's a gap in the first lane of traffic, the one by the curb. A small gap, maybe five seconds before the next bicycle. Then they just step out and start walking, and the riders in each lane slow down or swerve to avoid them. So long as their progress is predictable, no one hits them."

"I don't believe you," said Lynn. So we waited and watched until a fourth pedestrian crossed the street.

"We can do this," I said.

"No, we can't!" said Lynn. "You don't live here. You've only seen four people do it. You're going to get us killed."

"The drivers won't hit us," I insisted. "They're expecting people to cross the street, they know what to do."

The street in Hanoi

Holding Lynn's arm, I waited for the smallest gap and stepped into the traffic. "Come on," I said. "Stay with me." Lynn resisted for a moment, but she trusted me, and slowly and steadily she let me guide her through the stream of cars.

Step by step, side by side, we suppressed our fear and made it safely across.

Now, it was Lynn's turn to hold my hand and guide me to safety.

"You need someone safe to talk to," she said. "Someone with whom you can share these feelings without worrying about dragging me down."

Besides her monthly lung cancer support group, Lynn had a therapist, a woman named Sharon whom she'd seen for years; when they couldn't meet in person, they talked by phone. That weekend I began looking for a therapist of my own. I spread the word among our close friends and asked for recommendations. Eventually, I arranged appointments with three different therapists who accepted my insurance, hoping I would be comfortable with one of them.

By the time I found someone I liked, my ribs had healed, and I was feeling much better. I had expected to choose a woman, as I've always felt more comfortable talking to women, but one of the therapists was a man who came highly recommended. I left a message on his phone machine: "Hello Frank, you don't know me, but I was referred by your colleague Jean. I'm not in crisis now, but I was a few weeks ago, and my wife has stage IV cancer so I'm sure it will happen again, at least when she dies and maybe before. I'm looking to start therapy now, while things are calm, so we can get to know each other and build a relationship before everything goes bad."

Frank told me later, laughing, that this was one of the strangest phone messages he had ever received: so clinical and precise while describing a crisis to come. We scheduled an appointment, and I clicked with him immediately. I started seeing him every Wednesday on the way home from work.

Frank supported me through Lynn's treatment, and we continued meeting for two years after she died. No matter how bad things were, I always had someone to confide in and never again felt so alone.

↶

Lynn is taking multiple pain meds, but all they do is make her sleepy. She does not leave the apartment except to go to appointments. She spends her days sleeping, drawing the cat, talking with friends, and looking at paintings they have posted on the web.

For the past ten months, Dr. Hellmann has prescribed Lynn's pain medications, but now he says the intensity and complexity of her pain is more than he, an oncologist, can manage. He thinks it's important Lynn have a single doctor to work with on pain management and recommends Dr. Chen, the anesthesiologist.

But Lynn has another idea. Recently, her lung cancer support group featured a presentation by a palliative care doctor from Mount Sinai, Bethann Scarborough, who was tremendously sympathetic. "Palliative care addresses the entire spectrum of a patient's physical and emotional pain," explained Dr. Scarborough. "It's not just about pills and injections. And cancer patients who start palliative care early in their treatment tend to survive longer and do better than patients who wait until they are close to dying." Lynn liked hearing this and asks Dr. Hellmann for a referral to Sloan's Palliative Care department.

At first, Dr. Hellmann is skeptical; he's always relied on anesthesiologists for pain management. But then he remembers a particular palliative care doctor, Alison Wiesenthal, whom he likes when they see each other at meetings. He says Alison, as he calls her, is "a little feisty," and asks Lynn if she'd be comfortable working with a feisty doctor. Lynn lights up; she loves to joke and spar with her doctors, so, of course, she says yes.

Wednesday, September 9, 2015
www.CaringBridge.org/LynnKotula

Lynn has been staying home because of pain and unsteadiness, but on Saturday we managed to walk around the block. You wouldn't believe how exciting a four-block walk in your own neighborhood can be! Emboldened, we got into a cab the next day and went grocery shopping at Fairway. I had to lift everything into the cart, but Lynn was able to walk around the store without much pain, though once home she had to lie down for hours to recover from the effort.

Tuesday changed everything. A friend who lives out of town accidentally bought too many tickets to *Hamilton*, the hit musical, for a family reunion, and asked us whether we'd like to go. This was too exciting to pass up.

The seats were in the mezzanine, which an usher helpfully announced was fifty-six steps up from the lobby.

Lynn climbed those stairs twice, grasping the hand-rail and using her cane for balance, while dodging the patrons in the sold-out theater. That's 112 steps total, up and down. It's amazing what the right incentive can do. During Lynn's physical therapy, she has barely felt comfortable going up and down five steps in the stair-well of our building. Now she's done twenty times as many with no problem because she was excited to see *Hamilton*.

We just need time. This type of fracture can take months to heal, and Lynn will need continuous pain medica-tion if she wants to move about and have a life. But if Dr. Wiesenthal can help us find the right cocktail, Lynn might be back in her studio in a matter of days.

Five days later we have a wonderful meeting with the pal-liative care team.

We first see a nurse practitioner named Nina. She comes into the room with two pages of printouts, which is a summary of Lynn's chart that she wants to discuss. No one else has prepared so thoroughly for a visit. Nina spends more than forty-five minutes asking factual ques-tions about Lynn's history as well as probing questions like, "How does having cancer make you feel?" and "What do you want to be able to accomplish while you have can-cer?" She is so nice, so gentle, and so on-the-mark with her questions and responses, Lynn later tells me she could have spent the entire day talking with Nina.

We also really like Dr. Wiesenthal and her nurse, Bethany. With bright shining eyes, Dr. Wiesenthal is quick-witted and playful. She has Lynn cut back on the opiates, which gives her more energy, but at the cost of some new pain and more trouble sleeping at night.

Over the next few months, Lynn tries several medications as well as acupuncture and medical marijuana, until we find a combination that allows her to get through the day with a clear head and a manageable level of pain. The specifics don't really matter; it's the relationships that keep you going, and Lynn comes to treasure her relationship with Dr. Wiesenthal and her team.

The palliative team sees Lynn differently than the other doctors do. They understand the complex relationships between Lynn's medications better than anyone else, and they will be the people we call first when managing a new side effect. Palliative care is a beautiful thing.*

◡

Lynn has two upcoming exhibitions, both of which require extensive preparation. As the pain recedes, she spends every possible minute in her studio, trying to get as much done as she can before things go wrong again.

Thursday, October 1, 2015
www.CaringBridge.org/LynnKotula

This week marks the one-year anniversary of the Sunday afternoon when Dr. Weinstein called, and our lives turned inside out. Sure, the cancer is alive in Lynn, and we are terribly aware that eventually it will beat the drugs, but that hasn't happened yet. We're both still here, closer to each other than we've ever been.

---

* Later, Sloan will rename their palliative care department to "Supportive Care" because too many people associate "palliative" with dying.

Lynn and I have entered an alternate reality in which learning that cancer is in Lynn's sacrum strikes us as good news because it explains the fracture, and we have no problem leaving that cancer untreated unless it causes more problems. It is a world in which simply feeling good is a big win, and the point of her treatment is to continue feeling good for as long as possible. A world in which being required to see Dr. Hellmann every three weeks no longer feels like an imposition but, rather, a comfort.

Sloan has become an emotional anchor as much as a place where Lynn receives treatment. Like so much else about this new world, I would never have imagined it a year ago.

Lynn and I talk frequently about how unsettling it is that she seems so outwardly healthy. Our friends take every opportunity to tell her how vibrant and alive she looks, but we never forget that cancer is in her body, visible in every scan, and actively trying to kill her.

The side effects come and go. By spring they've become so much a part of our routine that I no longer bother to write about them. When we speak of them, it is as if they were a group of somewhat annoying relatives, crashing in our apartment. We are learning, finally, to live with the cancer.

∽

Meanwhile, our friend Sue is dying.

I've been charting her decline every Monday night for the past three years. ALS is a progressive disease that disables your muscles, one group at a time. After she lost the use of her legs, Sue was able to drive herself in a motorized wheelchair, and several times I accompanied her to the theater, but those days are long gone. The disease moved to her throat and then her chest, where it began stealing her ability to breathe.

When Sue's voice was failing, I facilitated phone calls with her family, leaning close so I could hear her faint halting words, and then repeating them to the person on the other end of the line. Eventually, speaking and swallowing became impossible. Sue used her eyes to form letters into words by staring at a finicky computer screen that tracked her eye movements, and then a gastric feeding tube was surgically implanted in her belly so aides could pour liquid nutrition directly into her stomach.

Although Sue intended to activate hospice services, she never got around to it. Her energy waxed and waned, each scary dip followed by a resurgence, and the hospice binder sat unopened on a nearby table.

By May, there is little work for me to do when I visit; mostly, I stroke her arm and tell her how well Lynn is doing. But one Monday I arrive to find that Sue has reached a new level of fatigue. Her breathing is irregular, and she barely listens to me.

That night I call her son, Ben, an undergraduate at Georgetown University. "I'm not an expert," I say, somewhat nervously, "but I think your mother is dying. If you want to see her before she goes, I think you should come home now."

It is exam week, and I've surprised him. When I hang up, I'm not sure what he will do.

A few days later, Ben calls to tell me that his mother died on Thursday, and that he was with her at the time. He starts to cry and tells me I have given him the greatest possible gift.

Lynn and I go to the funeral, where I tell Sue's family and friends about her unquenchable spirit, starting with the gleam in her eyes when I learned of her disease and she said, "Tell me about it!"

Now that she is gone, I have my Monday evenings back, but our friend is no longer with us to light the way. Luckily, Lynn is healing well. Sue's guidance doesn't feel as necessary as it once did.

Then, in late August, Lynn starts to lose control of her legs.

COMPLICATIONS
OF SURGERY

August 2016

We're in Blairstown, enjoying our summer vacation, when Lynn realizes something is wrong.

It's not that she can't walk. We regularly take a three-mile walk together, including some steep hills that she ascends at an impressive pace. But increasingly, she feels uncertain on her feet, as if her legs are not entirely under her control. Also, and more visible to me, she struggles going up and down the stairs, moving slowly and clutching the banister.

All of this is unsettling. Lynn's CT scans and her most recent MRI are normal, her spine looks fine, and there's no new pain. What the heck is going on?

Back in the city, we raise the question with Dr. Chaft, who is covering for Dr. Hellmann. She scrolls through Lynn's medical chart and looks up, puzzled.

"Did you ever receive intensive radiation in your spine? I don't see it here."

"Yes," says Lynn. "But it was at Mt. Sinai, before I came to Sloan Kettering."

"Right. I think I know what's going on."

Dr. Chaft says Lynn may have "radiation induced radiculopathy," a progressive and irreversible handicap caused by spinal radiation. Until recently, patients who received intensive spinal radiation usually died within a few months because their cancer was already advanced. Now that more and more patients are living for years, oncologists are increasingly seeing this pattern of symptoms and are questioning the wisdom of using radiation to treat spinal tumors.

Though "radiculopathy" sounds like a silly Harry Potter curse, the words "progressive" and "irreversible" are downright scary. If this is indeed what's happening to Lynn, we are in deep trouble.

At the end of our meeting, almost as an afterthought, Dr. Chaft pauses at the door and says, "Oh, by the way, your cancer is stable."

It's all so frustrating. Everything we're dealing with is a direct result of Lynn's treatment, not the cancer. In the short run, these impressive treatments have saved her life; in the long run, it's the treatments themselves that are doing the most damage.

The weakness in Lynn's legs worsens to the point where she starts using a cane again, and then a walker, though through sheer determination, she manages to climb the five flights of stairs to her studio. Coming back down turns out to be much harder.

We talk about this frequently. Has the radiation permanently damaged her spine? Will it worsen? Our lives

revolve around walking—together and apart, for pleasure and for errands, on level ground and up the stairs to
her studio. What will we do when Lynn can't climb those
stairs? How will she paint?

Once again, anxiety is in the air, made worse because
there doesn't seem to be anything we can do.

Then Lynn starts feeling numbness in her left foot and
toes. When she goes for her regular PT appointment, the
therapist is sufficiently concerned that he puts her in an
ambulance and sends her straight to Sloan's Urgent Care.
I drop everything to join her.

Lynn is seen almost immediately by an exceptionally
nice neurosurgeon with a soft southern accent. (Sounds
like an oxymoron, but not only does Lynn fall in love with
Dr. Bilsky, her nurse tells her to get in line because all the
nurses love him, too.) He asks her to walk down the corridor, then says to me, "See that? It's a drunken sailor's gait.
Her legs are swinging out instead of going straight."

Dr. Bilsky orders a spinal MRI, which reveals that
Lynn's spinal cord is being compressed by two of her vertebrae—exactly what we've feared all along. He puts her
on steroids and admits her to the hospital.

We do not speak with Dr. Bilsky after the MRI; all the
information comes from the urgent care staff. But it is
clear that one possible treatment is spinal neurosurgery.

Lynn wonders if she should get a second opinion, perhaps from someone at the Hospital for Special Surgery
across the street. So when I get home, I google Dr.
Bilsky. Turns out he is Sloan Kettering's vice chairman
for clinical affairs in neurosurgery and director of their
Multidisciplinary Spine Tumor Service—a world-class

expert on the treatment of spinal tumors, the kind of doctor people seek out for second opinions. We decide to wait and see what he has to say.

The next morning, I ride my bike to the hospital bright and early so I can be in Lynn's room when Dr. Bilsky stops by.

It is as we thought: "The MRI clearly shows spinal cord compression," he explains. "And your way of walking, the ataxic gait, is significant. I see several patients a year with this condition. No question about it, we need to relieve the compression and stabilize your spine."

Dr. Bilsky has scheduled the surgery for Monday afternoon, just two days from now, an indication of how serious this condition is. He says he will perform the surgery himself in what we later learn is his own dedicated operating room. He plans to "open up" the two vertebrae that are pressing on Lynn's spinal cord and implant a titanium rod to bridge the vertebrae above and below them. If all goes well, Lynn will head home at the end of the week.

All of this is a relief compared to what we had started to fear: irreversible radiation damage or perhaps a brain tumor. What a crazy situation we find ourselves in, where spinal surgery sounds good!

I call a friend and ask him to sit with me while we wait for the results. Until now, I've been on my own for all of Lynn's procedures, waiting either in the hospital or outside in the sunshine. Now I find that I don't want to be alone. I tell myself that nothing is going to go wrong, but I want to be distracted during the procedure and have support if something does.

Monday, September 19, 2016

In the morning a routine ultrasound shows blood clots in Lynn's left leg, which could be a serious problem during and immediately after surgery: If a clot breaks loose and moves into her lungs, it will become a deadly embolism. So Dr. Bilsky arranges for an interventional radiologist to implant a metal filter in the vein leading from her legs to her heart. It will be inserted via a catheter, threaded down from her neck, a procedure that takes about an hour.

They set everything up so that once the filter is in place, Lynn is wheeled directly to the surgical suite on the sixth floor, where Dr. Bilsky performs a "posterior lateral decompression and fixation" on her spine. Meanwhile, my friend Mark arrives to keep me company, and we grab some food at a Cuban restaurant across the street.

Surgery begins at 3:30 p.m. Three hours later, Mark and I are ushered into a small room where Dr. Bilsky enters from another door, still wearing his scrubs, and sits down facing us.

"The procedure went extremely well," he says. "We can monitor spinal activity in real time, and as soon as we screwed in the rod, more traffic started getting through her spine. Which was a bit surprising because I hadn't opened up her spinal cord yet. But I'll take it."

I ask if he knows what caused the compression.

"We're not sure. The substance pressing on her cord wasn't what we usually see. It's some kind of sludge, a combination of dead tumor cells, bone cells, maybe a bit of kyphoplasty cement. We've sent it to the lab for analysis."

Until Dr. Bilsky gets the lab results, there's no way to know whether active cancer is involved. If not, he says, the compression may end up being classified as "just one of those things." I've always liked that phrase, but it's a bit disconcerting coming from a neurosurgeon.

Dr. Bilsky plans to leave the metal filter in place indefinitely to avoid any risks involved in removing it, so Lynn won't need another one implanted the next time she has surgery. "Even though today went well," he cautions, "I'll probably see her again. That's what happens once cancer attacks your spine."

After he leaves, Mark and I sit for a few minutes processing these words.

The good news is that it looks like Lynn's spinal cord will start working, and she'll be able to walk, paint, and climb stairs. The bad news is that Dr. Bilsky expects to see her again. I think Bilsky is wonderful, but that's not what we want to hear. It's another reminder that Lynn is living on borrowed time.

A couple of hours later, I'm allowed to visit Lynn in the recovery room. This is disturbing and difficult. She is starting to come out of the anesthesia—disoriented, uncomfortable, and mumbling repetitively. She doesn't know where she is and thinks she is having a bad dream. "Make it stop," she says. "I want to wake up. Make it stop." But nothing I say seems to help.

I am almost relieved when the nurse kicks me out and tells me to come back tomorrow.

✺

On Wednesday they manage to get Lynn out of bed for two minutes, the first step towards her recovery. It takes a nurse, a physical therapist, and an occupational therapist to do it, and at a huge cost of pain and effort on Lynn's part. As soon as she gets back into bed, she falls asleep. Spinal surgery is no joke.

On Friday, Lynn makes her first walker-assisted foray outside the room. Two physical therapists accompany her: One puts a safety strap around her waist and walks beside her in case her legs buckle, while the other follows behind with a wheelchair. By Saturday, they trust her to use the walker on her own, so she and I take a couple of celebratory laps around the ward. On Sunday I am allowed to bring her home, where she is reunited with Jack, who curls up beside her and purrs loudly. This is truly the best therapy.

That evening we spend what feels like forever preparing a medication administration calendar for the next four weeks. I move furniture and clear a path so Lynn can safely move around the apartment and use the new commode I ordered from Amazon, which we position over our toilet to add much-needed height and safety handles.

Because of the clots in her leg and the potential for more, Lynn will take a blood thinner for the foreseeable future. At the hospital, they taught her to inject it into the soft flesh of her belly twice a day, and on Sunday afternoon she does it at home for the first time.

Lynn is on multiple pain killers and sleeps often, but with each passing day she seems better. We are both greatly relieved to have the surgery behind us, and I finally feel comfortable enough to go to the office again. Which lasts exactly one full day.

Tuesday, September 27, 2016

I am at work in Brooklyn, an hour away, when Lynn calls. "I can't move," she says, her voice shaky. "There's too much pain. You need to come home."

"What happened?"

"All I did was roll over." She is near tears. "I didn't twist or lift anything. It started all by itself. I don't understand."

It is barely lunchtime and I feel like I just got here, so I ask her to hang on until I get home.

"No! You have to come now. I need to pee, and I don't want to wet the bed."

I drop everything and rush home, where I find Lynn lying still as a statue on top of the bed, her hands clenched tightly at her sides. But I am too late; she has already peed on the floor beside the bed, leaving a puddle for me to mop up.

We call Dr. Bilsky's office and his nurse, Cynthia, says this sounds like nerve pain rather than something new, possibly caused by titrating Lynn off the steroids. She thinks Lynn is going through a short-term spike of major nerve pain, which should decline as her spinal cord heals.

For two days, the nurses try to find a combination of drugs to manage Lynn's pain without knocking her out. But trying to diagnose and treat her over the phone isn't working, so on Thursday Dr. Bilsky decides that she needs to come back to urgent care, where she can be seen and scanned.

The CT scan reveals nothing that would explain Lynn's pain. They decide to admit her so Dr. Bilsky can examine her, take additional images, and adjust her medications.

Unfortunately, the hospital upstairs is full. When I leave on Thursday evening, Lynn is lying on a cot in the hallway, but they promise her a bed upstairs as soon as that can be arranged, which we assume means later that night.

Lynn spends the next thirty hours in urgent care, much of it on a cot in a hallway. She is not alone: The hospital upstairs is at 110 percent capacity, and the hallway is full of patients waiting for beds.

I gather this is not uncommon. Sloan Kettering has grown greatly over the past decade, opening outpatient centers all over the region, but the hospital and its urgent care department have not significantly expanded. I am urged by two different nurses to submit a complaint on Lynn's behalf. "Perhaps if enough patients complain," says one, "the hospital will expand the UC [urgent care] and relieve the overcrowding."

We think a lot about this during those incredibly long, fatiguing, and frustrating hours in the hallway. There are twenty-one curtained alcoves in urgent care, which are eyed covetously by patients waiting in cots or wheelchairs, but those alcoves are used for initial examinations and for patients who need more serious attention. Lynn manages to score one when she first arrives, which allows her privacy, so hospital staff are willing to give her a bedpan. But when they take her for an ultrasound, she loses her spot and spends the rest of the day in the hallway, preoccupied with how and when to use the single bathroom. This includes strategizing when to ask for pain medication so she will get maximum relief during the few minutes needed to climb out of the cot, get to the bathroom, lower herself onto the toilet, and then reverse the process and get back to her cot. And also, strategizing when to flag down a passing nurse or aide to ask for help, since even with pain medication she can't manage those maneuvers on her own.

To pass the time, Lynn and I admire the tiny architectural details we can see from her cot: The way the walls meet the ceiling and the decorative panels above the kick rails. When her sister calls to commiserate, Lynn fills her in but then grins and says: "Well, it is a nice hallway!"

Saturday, October 1, 2016
www.CaringBridge.org/LynnKotula

Late last night Lynn was finally moved to a room upstairs in the neurology unit. Almost immediately she had her first pain-free half hour since last Monday. At 11:09 p.m., she texted me: "Pain is better. I'm cured!!!" and then at 11:35 p.m.: "Is it the increased steroid? I'm ready for a walk." When I saw the texts this morning, I was ecstatic, but Lynn soon told me that it was a short-lived reprieve. The pain is back, though she says the hospital bed feels like heaven compared to the cot downstairs, and when I get there, she'd like to try walking around the unit.

The current theory is that inflammation is causing the pain around Lynn's spine, which returned when she was titrated off the steroids. Yes, this is the same theory we heard last Tuesday, but that was over the phone. Then, they had a completely different theory on Wednesday. Now, they're back to the first theory.

Many thanks to those who dropped off food and flowers when we thought Lynn would be home to appreciate them. I've been slowly making my way through the food, relieved not to have to think about stocking the fridge.

~

For five days Lynn remains in the hospital while they try to relieve her pain. On the first day, the anesthesiologists inject a nerve blocker between her ribs, but it doesn't do much. Then for four days, they tinker with various levels of painkillers and send Lynn for scans that never reveal anything.

Most of the time, this is like an unusual, enforced vacation, punctuated by moments of severe pain and overshadowed by the fact that we haven't figured out how to get back to our normal life. The worst is when Lynn is positioned on an angle, trying to sit up or stand; the pain is excruciating. Once she is fully upright, it subsides a little but not enough for her to remain that way for long. When on her back, she feels fairly good.

Friends visit often, bearing flowers and gifts. Our friend Maja brings a large tub of Trader Joe's Dark Chocolate Peanut Butter Cups, to which Lynn quickly becomes addicted. "These work much better than the drugs!" she declares, as she reaches for another.

There is no solution and no explanation for the pain, just slow, steady, fractional improvement in Lynn's ability to manage it with medication. By the time she is discharged on October 7, she has spent seventeen of the past twenty-one days in the hospital.

At home Lynn is able to stretch out in familiar surroundings, with Jack the cat beside her. When she tells me she feels woozy, we assume it's the pain killers. It doesn't occur to us to take her temperature.

On Wednesday we go to our regular appointment with Dr. Hellmann. The first thing they always do is check Lynn's vital signs. Almost immediately, Dr. Hellmann's nurse, Maureen, comes over with a worried expression and two jars in her hands, each containing about an inch of murky fluid.

"You're running a fever," she says. "We need to take some blood cultures."

Maureen fills the jars with Lynn's blood so the lab can culture it for a possible infection, then gives Lynn some Tylenol to suppress the fever.

Lynn is surprised she has a fever but admits to having felt odd for the past few days. As we wait for Dr. Hellmann, her temperature rises to 101.5 and for a few minutes she seems confused about where we are.

They take fevers seriously at Sloan. As soon as Dr. Hellmann hears about Lynn's rising fever, he sends us straight to urgent care, where Lynn spends the night again, though this time in a curtained alcove rather than the hallway. We recognize many of the same staff members from our stint there last week.

They take blood tests, blood cultures, virus swabs, an X-ray, and a urine sample because they need to know what is causing the fever before they can decide whether Lynn can go home. But blood cultures take several days to get results and none of the other tests reveal anything.

At midnight, Lynn is transferred to the Clinical Decision Unit next door, which is a fancy name for a suite of overnight observation rooms on the first floor. It looks like a stage set for an upscale motel where the rooms (large curtained alcoves) all happen to have hospital beds.

Lynn's fever steadily drops and she seems less confused, though when I call the next morning she tells me that she spent the night thinking she was in Minnesota and asking her nurses what she was doing there.

∽

Lynn spends two days in the Clinical Decision Unit. On paper she is admitted to the hospital after her first night, but there aren't any beds upstairs, so here she stays.

The food isn't as good as upstairs (you get sandwiches and fruit cups, or whatever I can bring in from outside), and the beds are a lot less comfortable (the ones upstairs inflate and deflate rhythmically, like a gentle surf), but the nurses are friendly and they have a big jar of Halloween candy on the desk, which draws visitors from all over the building. Two nurses from the neurology unit stop in for a candy fix and are surprised to find Lynn here; they stay and chat for several minutes.

We haven't given a thought to Halloween, as it seems impossibly distant, but when the jar gets low, Lynn sends me out to buy several bags of candy to fill it up again.

Then one of the doctors arrives to tell us they've solved the mystery: The screws at the top of the titanium bridge in her back have come loose.

Friday, October 14, 2016
www.CaringBridge.org/LynnKotula

When Lynn is lying on her back, the screws fit into their holes and the bridge is positioned properly. In Lynn's CT scans, she is always lying on her back, so the hardware looks perfect. But when she sits or stands and leans even slightly forward, the screws slip out of the bone and the rod does not move forward, causing excruciating pain. I imagine the titanium rod pulling the screws out of her bone like nails in the claw of a hammer.

Dr. Bilsky tells us that in all his years he's never seen this. Screws sometimes come loose, but he was always able to see on a CT scan if a screw was floating or the hardware wasn't in the right position. Lynn spent three weeks in pain, including eight days in the hospital, because no one took a standing X-ray, until finally we came back for Lynn's fever and they grabbed a quick one in urgent care. And even then, many hours passed before someone noticed what was wrong. Surgery to replace the hardware is scheduled for Monday.

Lynn continues to run a modest fever, which is puzzling. She doesn't have any other symptoms of a systemic infection, and the surgical wound looks good.

Dr. Bilsky proposes that instead of spending the weekend in the hospital, we should go home until the surgery. All Lynn is doing is lying in bed and taking pain medications, which she can do just as well and more comfortably at home. He arranges for discharge early Friday afternoon and sends us home in an ambulance.

But we never make it into the apartment.

The ambulance lets us out in front of our building, leaving Lynn holding her cane in one hand and my arm with the other. Just inside the front door are three small steps up, which are usually not a problem, but when Lynn puts her weight on the first one, her knees buckle and she sinks to the floor. I try to hold her up, but I can't; she's off balance and too heavy. All I can do is slow her descent. She ends up half sitting, half lying against the vestibule wall, where she sobs quietly for a few minutes because she so desperately wants to be home.

Lynn remains on the hard stone floor for the next two hours, in too much pain to move, while I call Dr. Bilsky's office. They send another ambulance to take us back to the hospital.

Neighbors come and go. Some stop to ask what's wrong while others hurry by without looking. One goes upstairs and fetches several pillows, which we slide behind Lynn's back to ease the stress. For a while the doorman kneels beside her and holds her hand. Then it is back into an ambulance for the slow ride to the hospital in Friday afternoon traffic.

"Damn damn damn," writes our friend Naomi on CaringBridge that night.

"Worser and worser," says Libby, quoting the old Pogo comic strip, "and with that I date myself."

Saturday, October 15, 2016
www.CaringBridge.org/LynnKotula

After a rough night during which Lynn's fever spiked and she developed an irregular racing heartbeat (atrial fibrillation), she is back on the seventh floor, flying high on morphine while being closely monitored in the neurology ICU. Every now and then she opens her eyes and says a few words to me, some of which make sense, and then drifts off again.

This is the same floor where we were before, so we have a lot of friends among the nurses and aides here, several of whom stopped in to say hello. Lynn really does make friends wherever she goes, asking everyone about their personal lives, even while high as a kite and largely incapable of understanding their responses. She keeps checking email on her phone, but no one is writing, presumably because all her friends know she is high on morphine.

It's Saturday, things are quiet here, and you never know when the doctors will stop by. It is pleasantly, blessedly boring.

The boredom doesn't last.

That night Lynn's heart starts racing again, and her abdomen is uncomfortably distended, so they decide to postpone the surgery until Wednesday and spend the intervening days cleaning her out. She is put on a liquid diet and given multiple enemas and laxative injections that work exceedingly well: Over the next twenty-four hours, she has a series of messy accidents in, on, and beside the bed, terribly embarrassing her despite repeated assurances by Sparkle, the aide (so named for his multiple pairs of dazzling sneakers) that this is normal, don't worry, we're used to this.

The doctors think the atrial fibrillation is triggered by pain, so they increase her morphine. Before long she is disoriented and delusional. Her text messages start looking like butt-dials: "Moa icaon iland groaning all night long," "Rloolinhbhrg," "Mi... know u."

Then fluid starts building up around Lynn's lungs, and for a while the pulmonary team thinks this might have to be drained manually. Her blood oxygen level drops, so they put her on oxygen, and one night they even strap a mask on her face to force the oxygen into her.

Visiting her in this condition is hard, but she appreciates a familiar face as she drifts in and out of an eyes-open dream state. Some of what she says is disturbing (the nurses are conspiring to keep her here), while at other times, she is playful (the nurses are all pregnant and planning a group baby shower) and a bit of the old Lynn shines through.

On Monday, one of Lynn's blood cultures tests positive for an infection, and she is put on intravenous antibiotics. When the ICU nurse hears this, she claps her hands and says, "I knew it! When a patient is in pain and delirious, I always say, 'Find the infection; there has to be an infection.'"

These problems necessitate visits by what feels like every team of doctors in the hospital—cardiology, pulmonology, GI, internal medicine, infectious diseases, and psych, as well as the neurosurgeons—just about all of whom have to give their approval before Lynn can have surgery. Every hour another set of visitors wakes her up and asks the same questions.

Worst of all is Lynn's fear that she will never leave the hospital.

On Tuesday, Dr. Bilsky considers postponing the surgery again in order for the antibiotics to take effect. But then he decides that the risk of postponement is greater than the risk of operating while she has an infection.

Lynn hears him say this, but after he leaves I realize she doesn't understand. She grasps key fragments—another postponement, her body breaking down—and weaves them into a new narrative.

Tuesday, October 18, 2016
www.CaringBridge.org/LynnKotula

Lynn has been drifting in and out of the real world. Much of what she talks about consists of variations on how we need to plot together to get past those who are holding her here. (Not that she knows where "here" is, or why they are keeping her.)

The psych folks assure me it's common for patients in such circumstances to have delusions, and that they should dissipate once Lynn is out of pain and no longer taking morphine. They prescribed a modest dose of an atypical antipsychotic, which seemed to help last night and put her in a less worried state today.

Lynn's hands shake so much that she is unable to use her phone, which means she doesn't get to see the supportive emails from friends. This becomes another source of frustration, until she drifts into another world and it doesn't matter.

I spent much of the last two days trying to be a warm and reassuring presence, even though I wasn't sure how well everything was going. We're both extremely happy she's having the operation tomorrow.

15 comments

I, too, had what they called ICU psychosis. I told John, among other things, that my surgeon's sons were running up and down the halls (wrong hospital and he has daughters). I asked how many calories were in the glucose drip (it sounded like there'd be a lot!). I couldn't tell the difference between my dreams and reality. —Carmela

Wednesday, October 19, 2016

My friend Mark keeps me company during Lynn's surgery, a gesture that I appreciate even more the second time around. We sit together for almost five hours, distracting each other, talking about the challenges of running the restaurant he and his wife have inherited and the software system I am designing at work—the largest software project I've ever tackled.

When Dr. Bilsky finally enters the debriefing room, he looks puzzled and is shaking his head.

"When we removed the loose screws," he says, "we found puss in the screw holes, which is highly unusual. It appears to be infected with the same bug for which her blood tested positive, *E. coli* or something in that family, the sort of thing you might find in your gut. We spent a lot of time flushing her back with fluids before replacing all the hardware with a completely new set."

This is one more twist in what is already one of his more unusual cases.

Recovering from this, Lynn's second major spinal surgery in a month, is going to take a long time. The challenge is part physical, part psychological. Whenever anyone tries to get her to sit up I can see the flash of terror in her eyes, like a PTSD flashback, as she fights off her immediate, overwhelming fear of pain. I am immensely proud of her every time she overcomes this hurdle.

Monday, October 24, 2016
www.CaringBridge.org/LynnKotula

Lynn is on intravenous antibiotics and will remain on them long after she comes home. She now has two short

IV tubes dangling from the underside of her upper right arm; this is where we'll attach the antibiotic IV drips over the coming months. A nurse will come to the apartment each week to change the dressing. The only upside is that they no longer have to stick Lynn's hands and arms to draw blood; they attach to the IV tubes instead. Lynn's arms are thoroughly black and blue from all the attention they've received.

I thought our plates were full before, but this is a lot. Sometimes I look back at these posts and I can't believe we've been through so much. Luckily, most of the time, we just focus on the next step. The big picture will take care of itself.

Once again, I've avoided sharing the full truth with our friends. "This is a lot," I wrote, when what I really meant was, "This is a nightmare."

During these weeks I am overcome with fear, anger, frustration, and fatigue. I spend my days shuttling between the hospital and my job, which has locations in Brooklyn and upper Manhattan, as well as working from my home office and in the visitor's chair at the hospital. And on Tuesday evenings I reassure my mother: "Everything's fine, Mom. Lynn is doing well; she's had a few setbacks but she should be home soon."

Twice a week at the Manhattan location, I share an office with two therapists, and each time I see them they ask, "How's it going?" This triggers a thirty-minute monologue in which I unload everything that happened to Lynn since the last time I saw them. The words spill out, I can't help myself, but my colleagues are generous enough not to interrupt.

Every Wednesday I have a session with Frank, and for three weeks in a row the effect is the same: I walk into his office and start talking almost before he can ask me how I am, telling him the week's twists and turns, the nearly unbelievable story that I find myself living through. Sometimes I make it almost to the end of the session before Frank is able to ask a question.

And every few nights, I spend two or three hours writing a CaringBridge post, telling our friends about the most recent events. However, I always focus on what Lynn is going through and rarely write about myself.

Somewhere in between, I make dinner, do the dishes, feed the cat, and clean the litter box, although I'm not sure when that is—perhaps in the middle of the night while sleepwalking. The days and nights make about that much sense to me.

⌒

Before the second surgery, Lynn was delirious for five days, living in a world that was largely a figment of her imagination. After the surgery she seems better, and I assume the confusion is gone for good. But then, about four days later, it starts to happen again.

I am in Lynn's room, working on my computer, when she interrupts to ask where we are.

"What did you say?"

"Where are we?" she repeats. "What is this place? It seems very strange."

"We're in the hospital. Sloan Kettering."

"No we're not," she says. "Don't lie to me."

I hurry down the hallway and ask Lynn's nurse to come right away, but she doesn't seem concerned. "Oh, that's just hospital delirium," she says. "It's not uncommon when patients have been here for a while. They start to lose touch with their normal lives and invent a new reality."

"How come no one told me this before? I thought it would stop once she came off the morphine."

She shrugs. "It's not a big deal. It happens all the time."

But it feels like a very big deal to me. I thought Lynn was coming back to me, and instead she's gone somewhere else.

Lynn has a fantastic imagination, so she constructs a complex and interesting world. One day, there is a documentary on TV about bridges in Asia, and for hours, Lynn thinks that she and I are involved in designing and building bridges. Whenever people come into the room, she talks about those bridges, goes off on puzzling tangents, and asks questions about aspects of their lives that she has just invented. She does almost anything except the task at hand. It is challenging to know how to respond.

Lynn becomes aware of the many times I contradict her reality—telling her that events she vividly remembers never happened—and this terrifies her. She starts to think she is losing her mind and works hard to hide that fear from everyone but me. I am the lucky one, the person she trusts, and this means I have to constantly reassure her that everything will be okay, even though I, too, am terrified it won't.

Tuesday, October 25, 2016

In the morning, Lynn's nurse comes to find me and says they are planning to discharge her at the end of the week.

"I don't understand," I say. "Lynn can barely get out of bed and has only walked two feet."

"That doesn't matter. The doctors feel she'd be better off in a rehab facility, where she can have physical and occupational therapy for several hours a day. In a few weeks she should be strong enough to come home."

The idea of rehab conjures a host of unknowns: a facility that will be strange to Lynn, doctors and nurses we haven't met, and new systems and services I will need to understand. But the alternative— for Lynn to come home—would require me to arrange everything: physical and occupational therapy, home health aides, and a nurse to manage the IV antibiotics. It feels very difficult and expensive.

I ask Lynn what she would prefer, but she doesn't understand; I'm on my own for this. So I decide to follow the team's recommendation and send Lynn to rehab. It's a decision I will come to regret.

The hospital's social worker gives me a list of Medicare-approved nursing homes in Manhattan and tells me to choose five. Then he will send Lynn's referral material to those five and find out which, if any, will have a bed available on Friday.

That night I do a quick web search and discover that even the most highly-regarded nursing homes have some terrible reviews, so I write a post on CaringBridge asking whether any of our friends can recommend one. I receive lots of confusing and conflicting responses.

I do find one facility, Village Care, that seems to have better reviews, but it is far downtown and will be much harder for me to visit. I mention it to the social worker, and he adds it to the list.

On Thursday the social worker calls me. "A bed has just opened up in Village Care," he says, "and I strongly suggest you grab it. It might be gone tomorrow." Lynn's team feels there is no reason to wait until Friday. "We can see that she's slipping back into her fantasy world. Hopefully, getting her into rehab will help her snap out of it more quickly."

I hurry to the hospital, where I find Lynn both excited and confused. She can't stop talking about her impending departure, which she variously thinks is to go home with me, to go on vacation somewhere, or to go to a hotel in the West Village that she remembers thinking sounded good. She insists on getting dressed and sitting on the side of her bed an hour before the ambulance is due, like a kid before Christmas. But she can't sustain that position for long; the pain is too great. She lies down well before it arrives.

Thursday, October 27, 2016
www.CaringBridge.org/LynnKotula

Lynn is in room 203P at Village Care Rehab. The building is clean and new, the staff welcoming and friendly. If the only challenge now were Lynn's rehab, I would be happy.

Unfortunately, her delirium is on the rise again. She spent the late afternoon seesawing between clarity and confusion, moments of normalcy and moments when I wasn't sure she knew where she was or why. I am supposed to take it on faith that this is transient, but I have a hard time believing that.

Now that Lynn is stronger, I think she needs more contact with her normal life, by which I mean phone conversations and visits with friends. I strongly hope that each visit from someone Lynn cares about, and each conversation about events outside the hermetically sealed world in which she's lived for thirty of the past thirty-five days, will help her pull herself out of this mental fog and find her way back to us. That, little by little, reality will stick, and the fog will dissipate.

12 comments

I have seen hospital delirium before, and in both cases it resolved once they were home. I can only imagine how scary this must be for you! —Naomi

Because of the infection, Lynn is confined to a private room where she is isolated from the other patients; I have to put on protective gear to visit her. The isolation adds to her confusion, and as the days pass she becomes desperately unhappy, convinced she is trapped in some kind of prison.

As Lynn gains strength, it becomes increasingly problematic that she can't go out into the hallway or the dining room and is not allowed to use the rehab gym, where most patients receive their therapy. Instead, the PT and OT therapists come to her, and everything is done in her room. In theory, this should yield more focused sessions, but the therapists they send upstairs are the more junior ones, just out of school or still in training.

"That went well," I venture, after the first session.

"You don't know what you're talking about. I've had a lot more therapy than you. They barely know what they're doing." She's disappointed and angry, but it's the clearest sentence she's said all day.

The biggest problems are at night. Lynn's mattress is too firm for someone recovering from spinal surgery; she complains about it constantly and has trouble sleeping. She can't get out of bed without searing pain, and she is terribly afraid of soiling herself, especially overnight when there is only one aide per floor. I hire a private aide to sit in the room overnight, which seems to help, but I find myself spending every spare minute there (and a lot of non-spare ones).

While Lynn is in rehab, I try to see her twice each day. I rise early, work an hour at home before breakfast, and then ride my bike downtown to spend most of the morning with her, taking my laptop so I can work when she falls asleep. I leave before lunchtime to spend a few hours at one of our offices. Late in the afternoon, I take the subway back to Village Care, where I have dinner with Lynn every night. In the evening I take care of chores like shopping and laundry.

Friends visit throughout this period, often staying for dinner. Lynn doesn't like the food, so our friends Elizabeth and Mark introduce us to a nearby restaurant that makes pizza with wild mushrooms and truffle oil. Lynn loves it, and we order it again and again. It's thrilling to see her smile when she takes the first bite.

These are long days, made harder because Lynn does not understand where I go when I leave her. Each time I reach for my coat, she asks, "What do you think you're doing?"

"I'm going home. I have to feed Jack and get some sleep."

"Don't go. Stay with me. You can sleep here."

"I can't. I'd love to, but I have to do the shopping and clean the litter box and give Jack some love. He misses you so much."

"You don't really love me! If you did, you wouldn't leave me alone in this strange place."

It is bitterly difficult to go, but I have no choice. I have to hold the rest of our life together, and I have to get at least a few hours of sleep in our own bed.

∽

Slowly, day by day, Lynn gains strength. I learn more about how the rehab center is structured and build relationships with key staff members. We all spend a lot of time reassuring Lynn, and after about ten days, she finally has a good day.

"I had a very nice visit on Sunday afternoon," writes our friend Tony. "She was her usual social and gracious self."

"Bob and I saw Lynn together," says Monica, "and although she was a little distracted, she was still cracking jokes. When we asked her what we could bring, she told us to bring a hammer so she could knock out her fog!"

∽

Thursday, November 10, 2016
www.CaringBridge.org/LynnKotula

Yesterday, more than two weeks after she arrived, Lynn was finally allowed out of her room. This was tremendously exciting. She has been shuffling around the corridors with her walker, a huge smile on her face.

Lynn's mind is coming back, delusions mostly gone, but her thinking is foggy, and a lot of common words have gone missing. A few days ago, she forgot how to unlock her phone and couldn't get the hang of it even when I tried to show her; the concept of a password was gone. I suspect these gaps—and others like them—are cognitively related, and I'm sure they're temporary.

Now that she can think more clearly, Lynn feels lonely and bored, which also signals a big step forward. When she comes home next week, she is likely to be weaker than ever. We will need friends to visit and help her regain her walking strength. We also welcome gifts of food for at least a week or two.

Truthfully, I wasn't at all sure Lynn's cognitive losses were temporary and was desperately afraid they would be permanent. But I couldn't bring myself to admit that to anyone other than my therapist. Reassuring my friends of something I didn't believe was a way of reassuring myself, too.

At Last

Lynn is discharged from Village Care just before lunchtime.

It is a glorious day, both figuratively and literally. We take a taxi home in the bright sunshine, Lynn's window wide open, her face beaming in the light. Then we race around for an hour filling prescriptions and eating a bite of food before taking another taxi to see Dr. Hellmann and Maureen, whom we greet like long-lost friends.

Dr. Hellmann is extremely solicitous. He has prepared a chart of the different goals we need to reach to get Lynn back to where she was a few months ago. For the first time, it occurs to me that what Lynn went through in the hospital—and continues to go through—is deadly serious. Though neither he nor anyone else has said it in so many words, Dr. Hellmann implies that the infection could easily have killed her, and it sounds as if he is not sure she will ever regain her strength.

"Your rehab is the most important goal," he says. "Everything else depends on it."

Saturday, November 19, 2016
www.CaringBridge.org/LynnKotula

When Lynn was in the hospital, I was so focused on supporting her that I missed what was staring me in the face. Even while slogging through the long days and dealing with all the issues that kept coming up, it didn't occur to me that she might die. But that blindness served me well because I was never deeply scared during those weeks, never paralyzed. Every day I came home exhausted and spent hours telling my colleagues how angry and frustrated I was, but I always wanted to get back to Lynn, as there was always something else that needed to be done.

Coming home has not been as straightforward as we'd hoped. Lynn is weaker than we realized and unable to perform many of the household tasks she looked forward to. At times, especially when tired, she gets depressed and wonders whether she will ever regain her strength. It's a recurring theme in our conversations. I tell her that every day she is stronger than the day before. Sometimes she believes me, sometimes she doesn't.

There are still cognitive gaps, too. I am glad the psychiatrist at Village Care told us these symptoms can linger for four to six weeks after the primary delirium. Lynn doesn't remember that conversation, so I have to keep reminding her of it, too.

11 comments

Thank you both for allowing us to share in the journey. And clearly, this last part has been arduous. —Naomi

Welcome home, Lynn. One minute at a time . . . —Ann

There's NO place like HOME! Your kitty will love it! Sending Love and Light to my two WARRIORS! —Nancy

At home we are surrounded by boxes of medical supplies for the IVs, anti-coagulants, and the weekly blood draw. We have learned to administer the daily injections and infusions like the pros that we are. We even have a bright red "Sharps" container into which I drop the used syringes. A nurse comes once a week to clean the intravenous line and change Lynn's dressing, otherwise we are on our own.

The cost for all this: about $1,000 in co-payments so far. These meds and services would have been fully covered had Lynn remained in the rehab facility, but at home we have to pay for them, which is ridiculous since it is clearly in everyone's best interest for her to be home. Luckily, we can afford it, at least for a while.

Tuesday, November 29, 2016

When Lynn's course of IV antibiotics is almost over, we go to see the infectious disease specialist who prescribed them.

Dr. Sejal Morjaria is a tall woman in her thirties who is by far the coolest doctor we've met at the hospital, and the only one who didn't wear a white coat when she came to see Lynn. The way she strode through the halls reminded me of an old-time gunslinger. It was Dr. Morjaria who analyzed Lynn's infection and designed the unique combination of antibiotics to attack it.

Dr. Morjaria makes a point of repeatedly saying, "You look amazing. Your labs look amazing," which we find hard to believe because Lynn is still pale and shuffling around, but apparently she looks a lot better than when Dr. Morjaria last saw her. She gives Lynn permission to stop taking the IV antibiotics and switch to less expensive medications instead.

We wait another week to make sure nothing terrible happens and when nothing does, a technician arrives to remove the intravenous tubes dangling from Lynn's armpit, and we pack up all the supplies. Lynn's particular flavor of *E. coli* doesn't respond to any known oral antibiotics, so removing the tubes is a major step, but enough weeks have passed that Dr. Morjaria is confident the infection is gone for good.

Lynn is desperate to stop giving herself the twice-daily blood-thinner injections, so Dr. Hellmann refers us to a hematologist who agrees to switch her to an oral blood thinner. This is especially good financially because due to Medicare's "donut hole"—the gap in prescription drug reimbursement—refilling Lynn's injection prescription would have cost more than $1,000 for the next month's supply, whereas the oral medication "only" costs us $165. And this is with good insurance!

When Lynn was in the hospital, I posted almost daily, but now that she's home the urge comes less often. My tone changes, too. You can sense my relief as I realize that Lynn is finally getting better.

Sunday, December 18, 2016
www.CaringBridge.org/LynnKotula

Wow, almost four weeks have flown by. The commode that sat over our toilet and the plastic chair that filled our bathtub are now in storage.

Lynn saw Dr. Hellmann again who described her recovery as "profound." These types of comments keep surprising us. We truly did not realize how ill she was.

About two weeks ago, Lynn started bantering with me. I didn't realize how much I missed sparring with her until it came back. I feel like we're a couple again, rather than patient and caregiver.

We went to a museum today, taking the walker on the bus. It was Lynn's first nonmedical outing since September. When she first came home from rehab, she slept twelve to fourteen hours each night, plus two to three hours in the afternoon. But now she's down to ten hours each night and maybe a one hour nap, or sometimes no nap at all. And still, no sign of cancerous activity!

A few weeks later, we learn that Lynn's childhood friend Nancy has died.

For months Nancy has driven us crazy with her ALL-CAPS comments on CaringBridge, written in a pep-rally style unlike anyone else's, featuring greeting card sentiments like "WE WILL FIGHT ON" and "TOGETHER FOREVER," as well as an unusual willingness to share intimate details, as if she were writing privately to Lynn rather than posting on our blog. Nancy's comments often embarrassed us, and her insistence on using the "fight" metaphor clashed with our desire to describe Lynn's treatment as an ongoing learning process. But the embarrassment was clearly our problem, not hers. Nancy was just being herself.

The news of Nancy's death comes as a shock. We knew she had stage IV cancer, so it isn't a surprise, but we didn't realize how much she meant to us. Belatedly, we discover that her words of encouragement, her out-there, politically-incorrect openness, the sense that she and Lynn were in this together, touched us more than we knew. That night I write a CaringBridge post acknowledging our loss. Sometimes you don't realize how much someone means to you until they are gone.

∽

Saturday, February 11, 2017
After six weeks of discussion with Dr. Hellmann and an extensive round of testing, Lynn drops out of the clinical trial.

This is huge. Almost twenty-seven months have passed since Lynn's first infusion. Although we originally expected the trial to stop after two years, it turns out they can't drop you while the experimental drug may be what's keeping you alive. Lynn is leaving voluntarily.

It also represents a huge vote of confidence from Dr. Hellmann.

"By now you've received whatever benefit the immunotherapy is going to give you," he says. "The longer you take it, the more you risk a potentially devastating autoimmune reaction. Better to quit while you're ahead."

Going forward, there will be no more infusions, just a daily Tarceva pill before breakfast. Lynn will no longer go to Sloan every three weeks, no longer get a CAT scan every six weeks, and no longer spend an extra five hours at the outpatient center every time she sees Dr. Hellmann. Fewer needle sticks, fewer scans, more of her life back.

When Dr. Hellmann first raised the idea of dropping out of the trial, Lynn felt ambivalent. Her frequent visits to Sloan Kettering made her feel safer, as if simply being there kept the cancer at bay. But the more she thought about it, the more she realized that she wants to spend her remaining years doing something more meaningful than going to medical appointments. "It will be good to have a longer gap between appointments and scans," she tells me. "More time to paint and cook and see my friends."

Unfortunately, dropping out of the trial means we must start paying for Lynn's Tarceva, which will cost about $5,000 per year (after insurance). The first $2,500 is due this month.

Maureen tells us that the drug companies offer financial assistance; if we qualify, we can get the Tarceva for free. Eligibility is based on the proportion of our income that we spent on medical expenses the previous year.

Last year (2016) the clinical trial paid for Lynn's cancer medications, so our medical expenses were relatively low. When we fill out the application, we realize that the few thousand dollars we spent on blood thinners and medical supplies aren't enough for us to qualify. We will have to pay for the Tarceva for the rest of 2017.

In 2017, Tarceva costs so much that we *do* qualify for assistance in 2018, so in 2018 the Tarceva costs us nothing. But that means we won't qualify for assistance in 2019.

It's a crazy system. Every second year we qualify for financial assistance, but receiving it means we won't qualify the following year.

In 2018, we figure this out, so Lynn buys some prescription hearing aids. We've known for years that she needs hearing aids, but she didn't want to spend the money when she didn't know how long she had left to live. Now the very fact of buying them qualifies us for enough financial assistance that they're effectively free.

Like so much else in the American health care system, this is completely nuts. But Lynn enjoys her fancy new hearing aids, which are especially helpful in the crowded gallery openings that she loves to attend.

ᔆ

The year 2017 is a good one, our first since Lynn's diagnosis. She gets steadily stronger while the tumors remain unchanged. I only write one more post the entire year, in June, titled "No News is Good News."

The back pain remains, but Lynn manages it with a modest dose of OxyContin, the extended-release opioid designed specifically for chronic pain.

Lynn could be the poster child for OxyContin: Once she becomes accustomed to it, she never seems to get high, never wants to increase her dose, and it does a beautiful job of holding down her pain. Every month she gets another bottle of sixty pills, which she takes twice a day, one in the morning and one at night.

The palliative care team assures Lynn that this is safe; she is chemically dependent on OxyContin and will suffer withdrawal effects if she stops taking it, but she is not "addicted" in the sense of needing to take increasing amounts to get through the day. And opioids work better and have fewer side effects than Tylenol or Advil because they're kinder to the liver and stomach lining. It is a perfect fit for Lynn.

Unfortunately, millions of other people are finding ways to abuse OxyContin, and in 2017 the drug becomes synonymous with the overdose crisis. States start passing rules to limit its use, and chain pharmacies stop carrying it.

Lynn has been filling her prescriptions at Duane Reade, a New York City chain with a location near our apartment, but each month the pharmacists take longer to fill her order, and then for two months in a row she spends hours calling around to find a Duane Reade location that has OxyContin. This is frustrating, time-consuming, and clearly unsustainable.

She decides to try a local pharmacy that is not part of a chain, but when Lynn presents her prescription, the pharmacist refuses to fill it. "I'm not willing to support your addiction," he says harshly. "You need to stop taking this."

Lynn tries to tell him about her constant pain and the success she's had with OxyContin, but he doesn't want to hear it. He makes her feel dirty and small, and she resolves never to go there again.

When Lynn tells the palliative care team about these problems, they suggest a pharmacy that processes many of Sloan's prescriptions and delivers opioids by bicycle all over Manhattan. This works like a charm. Lynn develops a strong phone relationship with the pharmacy staff, and when we stop in to meet them in person, we are surprised to find that it is a small, privately-owned neighborhood pharmacy that looks like any other. But it serves a crucial need for the many Sloan Kettering patients who rely on opioids to manage their pain.

As Lynn gains strength, our cat, Jack, who has probably done as much as any drug to ease Lynn's pain, is slowly losing his.

We have been keeping Jack alive with steroids for more than two years, ever since he lost half his weight, and the vet decided that he probably has a tumor in his sinus cavity. When we told her we weren't able to pay for expensive scans or extraordinary measures, she suggested steroids to shrink the tumor and ease his pain.

The steroids worked brilliantly, and Dr. Venezia prescribed them for longer than she would have a healthy cat. We knew Jack was living on borrowed time, but we loved him all the more for it.

In March, the steroids stop working and Jack's tumor gets the upper hand. For a few weeks we watch his body shut down and he loses interest in life. When he is no longer able to eat or climb onto the bed or do any of the things he loves, we decide the time has come.

At the vet, we stroke Jack and try not to let him know how sad we are as we say goodbye. Then Dr. Venezia injects two drugs: the first to induce a gentle sleep, the second to stop his heart.

When we get home Lynn says she doesn't want to replace Jack. It's the first time in twenty-five years that we haven't had a cat in our lives, but she can't imagine investing her love in another one when the future is so uncertain.

I understand her reluctance, but it's sad to come home to a truly empty apartment, and I miss the soft patter of Jack's feet and the warmth of his body on the bed.

As the months pass, Lynn grows steadily stronger and her optimism grows, until one morning she surprises me by saying, "I'm ready now. I want to feel a cat in my arms again."

Dr. Venezia's office runs a small animal shelter. We call and ask whether they have any female gray tabbies, since these have always been Lynn's favorite. "Yes," they say, "one just came in, but she's part of a pair. If you adopt her, you will also have to adopt the big black male who came with her."

We hurry to the office to see them. The receptionist ushers us into a small exam room where we sit on the floor, waiting.

After a minute a technician brings in two kittens, big fluffy Boo and sleek petite Lily. Immediately they walk toward us. Boo comes straight to me and starts rubbing against my leg, while Lily unerringly targets Lynn, jumps into her lap and begins to purr.

Monday, January 1, 2018
www.CaringBridge.org/LynnKotula

These past six months have been wonderful. Lynn only has a few hours of energy per day, but she makes good use of them.

After such a long series of unchanging scans, we no longer obsess about Lynn's cancer and instead focus on the side effects, the small stuff. Recently, one of those side effects—an uncomfortable acne that pops up in all sorts of intimate places—has been getting worse, and Lynn spent months shuttling between Sloan doctors trying to mitigate it. Then Dr. Hellmann told Lynn that he wanted to switch her to a newer drug called Tagrisso. It works much like Tarceva but has a lower incidence of side effects, including acne. While we are both nervous to switch cancer medications, Lynn is excited at the possibility that she will stop looking like a pimply-faced teenager who happens to have wrinkles.

In one of my early posts, I wrote that the name of the game is to buy time: Science moves quickly, and new treatments will come along if Lynn can hang in there long enough. This appears to be happening now.

To sum up: We're here, excited and nervous, learning to make the best of what we've got, and looking forward to an even better 2018. And did I mention our two beautiful kittens?

In the spring our friend Carmela, who has written so many helpful—and funny!— CaringBridge comments, undergoes heart surgery.

Carmela has Marfan syndrome, a genetic disorder that disrupts the connective tissue in her body. She's already endured several major heart operations; now, she needs another.

The surgery goes well. John, her husband, sends word that she is recovering, and we all breathe a sigh of relief—until suddenly, a week later, something breaks inside her, and she dies quickly.

When Lynn and I attend the wake, we are struck by how shattered John seems. He can't stop talking about how well Carmela was doing after the surgery, how he was sure the worst was behind them. Even though he has lived with Carmela's disease for years, he was clearly unprepared to lose her and has no idea what to do next.

A few months later, we are invited to a memorial dinner, a catered affair on which John has spent considerable money. Each guest receives a copy of a beautiful color catalog of Carmela's art and an article of clothing (ties for the men, scarves for the women) printed with images from one of her paintings. John is giving each of us a piece of Carmela so we can have her with us forever. He is making sure her memory will live on, in our closets and on our bookshelves, and therefore in our hearts.

At the time, Lynn and I think this is excessive, a lot of money for something as ephemeral as a tie or scarf. How little we understand what it feels like to lose your beloved partner! A few years later, I will do something similar for Lynn.

∽

For two years, the Tagrisso holds down Lynn's cancer and we have a wonderful run.

Lynn no longer goes swimming (the rods in her back put an end to that) and we no longer travel anywhere (she always wants to be within an hour of her doctors), but within those constraints, we are able to do most of the things we love.

Lynn spends hours at a time in her studio, creating dozens of paintings that please her and sell well. She goes to museums and gallery openings all over the city, where she and her friends laugh together and share stories about art and life.

Lynn and a friend at Lynn's gallery

During spring and fall migration, we go birdwatching with friends in Central Park. We continue to enjoy long hikes on twisting trails, and on New Year's Eve we dance until well past midnight.

At work, I finish my big software project. Colleagues I barely know stop me in the hall to tell me how thankful they are and that my system has greatly improved their lives. It's a wonderful high.

The side effects come and go. One of them has given Lynn curly hair, which she always wanted. Now she thinks she looks great, and when she walks down the street in her signature red Canadian Mounties cap, strangers compliment her because no one has ever seen one quite like it.

On July 4, we attend a potluck celebration near Blairstown at a converted rooming house with a huge wraparound porch. While Lynn is occupied elsewhere, our friend Sue comes up to me and says, "Let's take a walk," so we step off the porch into the trees.

Sue's husband, a painter named Arthur, has Parkinson's disease. When Lynn and I first noticed tremors in his hands, maybe five years ago, we wondered whether it was Parkinson's but were afraid to ask; we figured he would tell us in his own time. But he never did. The tremors became more pronounced, and one day Sue admitted that she herself didn't know what was happening: Arthur had gone to his doctor but wouldn't tell her.

"He's a very private man," she said. "This isn't the sort of thing he shares with me."

This astounded us. "If they don't talk about something like that," Lynn said that night, "what do they talk about?" A stark reminder that you never know what binds a couple or makes their marriage work.

A few years later, Arthur told us that yes, he had Parkinson's, but he didn't want to treat it. "It's not curable," he said. "What's the point of taking all those drugs if they won't cure it?" We had to lean in close to understand him. His voice, always soft, was further muffled by the disease.

Now, strolling through the trees with distant laughter in the air, Sue tells me that she and Arthur have reached a better place: They've found good doctors, and Arthur has come to understand that the drugs and other therapies, including acupuncture and meditation, enable him to enjoy life. Best of all, he is still able to make beautiful drawings. The tremors don't affect him when he's holding a pen and concentrating.

It seems to me that Sue led him to this place, and I ask her how she managed to do that and at what cost.

"It's been hard," she says. "Much harder than I expected." She shares details about their days, the physical and emotional toll, the devastating panic attacks that are a common side effect of the disease. For much of the year, she and Arthur are alone together in their house in the woods. Arthur no longer drives, so Sue takes him everywhere and is his full-time caregiver.

Sue isn't looking for sympathy. She wants to share her story with someone who has walked this road before, someone who won't judge or question her, someone who understands.

As she speaks, it dawns on me that I've become that person.

The cancer is still with us, of course, a time bomb we do our best to ignore. We've become good at that. Every three months, Lynn has a CT scan followed by an appointment with Dr. Hellmann. The scans and appointments become part of the fabric of our lives, like an annual physical or seeing the dentist twice a year. We know in the back of our minds that this can't last, but it's impossible to be afraid when life is so rich and the end nowhere in sight.

A few years later, a friend with Stage IV cancer will post a list of sixteen "cancer lessons" that she's learned, several of which remind me of those three good years with Lynn:

I am strong enough to handle whatever life brings.

I can live with uncertainty.

My negative thoughts are normal.

I am able to ask for help.

I have nothing to fear.

I am loved.

Lynn in her favorite red hat

In the years since Peter died, Lynn and I have lost friends to ALS, cancer, and Marfan syndrome. We go to their funerals and mourn them, but we are no longer deeply weighted by each loss. They remind us, paradoxically, that we've drawn a lucky card. Within the context of Stage IV cancer, this is as good as it gets.

Living with cancer has brought us closer together: We are stronger, more supple, like two trees that can bend in the fiercest wind. Now we often hold hands when we walk down the street, and in 2019 we celebrate Valentine's Day for the first time.

"We're so lucky," says Lynn, as she touches her glass to mine.

"Yes," I agree. "We are."

Then, in January 2020, a routine scan shows that one of her lung tumors has doubled in size.

PART TWO

DYING

When does dying begin? Unless you are in an accident or have a heart attack, this is rarely an easy question to answer. Some say we begin dying the minute we are born.

I think Lynn began dying in January 2020, when her cancer started to beat the drugs and her body began to fail. This process played out over more than a year, and for most of that time we certainly did not think she was dying. We saw this as a new set of problems to solve—just as, five years earlier, we had overcome the hurdles posed by Lynn's initial diagnosis.

Almost until the end, we continued to hope another solution could be found, and this colored everything I wrote (or chose not to write) during that difficult year.

History Rhymes

Wednesday, January 8, 2020

Lynn has read the radiology report and asks me to accompany her to the meeting with Dr. Hellmann. Over the years, they've developed a lively rapport, can even be silly with each other, but not today. Gently he says, "Well, we've had a good run, but we knew this would happen sometime," which I find deeply unsettling even though I know it is true.

Then he hands us a lifeline. "It's only grown three centimeters," he says. "It's still quite small. Maybe if we wait, it will shrink back down. I've seen that happen before."

So we wait for the next scan, three months away, trying to ignore our growing anxiety. This is torture and colors our every waking moment. Lynn complains about shortness of breath, as if the tumor has compromised her breathing. Then, in February, she feels a new pain in her back and shoulder. Dr. Hellmann takes this seriously, pushes up the date of the next CT scan and orders a full-body PET scan to go with it.

In March we get the results: one tumor has continued to grow, but the other two remain unchanged. Dr.

Hellmann suggests we radiate it while continuing to use Tagrisso to hold down the others. Hopefully this tumor is an outlier and not a sign of worse to come.

The scans don't explain Lynn's pain, however, and the tumor is too small to affect her breathing. Dr. Hellmann suggests that her symptoms may be caused by anxiety layered on top of the extremely small physical changes, a diagnosis we are happy to accept.

In mid-March, as the city shuts down for COVID, Lynn receives three days of targeted radiation on the growing tumor. In the waiting room, there is a bell on the wall, which patients are encouraged to ring when they complete their course of radiation. While we are there, a woman emerges from the treatment area and rings the bell three times. Everyone in the waiting room, patients and staff, clap and cheer. It is her end point, the day she's been waiting for.

The celebration makes Lynn uncomfortable. "I'm never going to be able to ring that bell," she whispers to me. Her three days of radiation are just a blip in a course of treatment that can never stop.

By the third day, the city is in full COVID lockdown, so I am not allowed to accompany Lynn. But afterwards, she is in good spirits, the side effects are minimal and only last a few days. Dr. Gomez, the radiation oncologist, warns us about some possible long-term side effects, including a pseudo-pneumonia called pneumonitis. But he assures us that it can easily be treated with steroids, and we don't think much about it.

᠀

April is another good month, in hindsight the last one Lynn will have.

The city is locked down, ambulances scream through the streets day and night, and temporary morgue trucks are parked outside hospitals, but somehow we are able to ignore it all. During Lynn's years of treatment, we grew accustomed to being an isolated pod of two; COVID means that now everyone else is doing it, too.

Every day we walk together on Riverside Drive, a tree-lined boulevard near the apartment, and marvel at how closely we are able to observe spring coming on, bud by bud and leaf by leaf. And at seven each evening, we lean out the window banging pots and pans to celebrate the essential workers who are keeping the city alive.

Soon Lynn returns to her studio, crosses the eerily empty Columbia campus, and climbs those five flights of stairs to work on a painting. Once there, she needs to rest before she can start, but she is painting, and that's what matters.

In May, Lynn's energy starts to drop. Instead of walking, she takes the bus to the studio, where she finds it harder to climb the stairs and has to stop for breath partway up. Within a week, she is too tired to go at all. She stays in bed most of the day for the first time in years.

It's all very puzzling since she has no symptoms other than extreme fatigue— no fever, cough, or shortness of breath associated with COVID. But we don't think it's cancer, either. She had a set of scans just two months ago; it seems impossible that the cancer could be beating the drugs so soon.

After a couple of days, I convince Lynn to go to the hospital to be examined. She doesn't want to because she associates Sloan with all the dreadful things that happened to her there—the trauma is still very much alive. But crippling fatigue can't be ignored.

It turns out that Lynn has "organized pneumonia," an aggressive form of the side effect Dr. Gomez warned us about. Her lungs are full of fluid and her oxygen level is down to 80 percent, a scary number, similar to what we are hearing about people with severe COVID.

Lynn is immediately hospitalized and put on a course of steroids and antibiotics. I'm not allowed to accompany her, so we stay in touch by phone and worry that she will catch COVID in the hospital.

When Lynn is discharged, five days later, we decide to move to Blairstown to shelter from the pandemic. We think the worst is behind us, and the country air will do us good.

For a while Lynn seems to improve. She is too weak to hike, but we assume this is a result of the pneumonitis and the drugs she is taking. I ride my bike on country roads and do all the shopping; Lynn alternates between painting and taking short naps with Lily.

She leaves the house just once each day, in late afternoon, for our daily walk. No more exploring paths and trails together, as now they have to be smooth concrete. We find a road that winds through extraordinary scenery and drive there every evening to look at birds and watch the sunset. Here, Lynn is cheerful and social; she starts chatting with neighbors on their evening walks, anticipates seeing them again.

In July, Lynn starts to feel more pain, first in her spine and ribs, then extending into her pelvis. She starts using a cane again, and a friend loans us a stack of pillows to cushion our hard wooden chairs. Her doctors try tweaking the palliative meds, but when that doesn't work, they order a battery of scans and tests. Soon we are driving back and forth across northern New Jersey to Sloan's satellite locations. Once again, cancer consumes our lives.

In early September we get the results, and it is all bad news: There are several new tumors in Lynn's spine and some larger ones in her pelvis. Clearly, the Tagrisso has stopped working. If we don't find another solution soon, the cancer will be unstoppable. We come back to the city, so Lynn can have a fresh biopsy and start a new course of treatment.

These days remind us all too vividly of 2014, when we first learned of Lynn's cancer. We are starting over, as if with a new disease. We spend hours traveling back and forth to Sloan's new outpatient facility near the East River. We can no longer walk through the park to get there, and Lynn is disappointed that the new building feels like an airport lounge. But the waiting rooms have spectacular views of the river, and there is a good cafeteria too.

I don't write any posts during this period, though not because there is nothing worth saying. Everyone we know is consumed with news about COVID and the US elections, and their lives have already been turned upside down by the virus. Our problems don't amount to a hill of beans by comparison, and isn't this a story we've told before? Only the details have changed.

At least, that's what we tell ourselves.

Honestly, I think we are afraid to admit how much is going wrong. We have a hard time restarting CaringBridge because doing so would make the danger to Lynn feel that much more real to us. So we muscle through our fear and anxiety, the endless cycle of appointments, tests, and decisions, without the help of our friends.

৲

In late September, Lynn experiences debilitating back pain; several more of the vertebrae in her lower back have collapsed. Dr. Bilsky recommends a set of kyphoplasties, the same procedure Lynn had twice in 2015. But she is hesitant— scared, in fact. In the intervening years, she has been traumatized repeatedly, first by the spinal surgeries and then by the delirium. Now, she is terrified that anesthesia might trigger more delirium.

We discuss this possibility with Dr. Hellmann, who reminds Lynn how well the first kyphoplasties worked for her, but still she hesitates. That afternoon I'm preparing for a video session with Frank, my therapist, when Lynn says she'd like his opinion, too. With Frank's agreement, I bring the phone into the bedroom and sit beside Lynn, holding it in front of us. It is the only time Lynn and Frank, each of whom has heard a great deal about the other, will see each other's faces.

Frank walks Lynn through a series of questions: "What exactly is a kyphoplasty? How does it feel to have one? What did they do for you when you had them before?" After a few minutes Lynn decides that yes, she does want another one.

Almost twenty years ago, Lynn and I traveled with a guide in rural Laos and stayed for several days in a small village. One day they took us on a hike to a nearby valley that involved walking through a kilometer-long cave with lamps strapped to our heads. The first few hundred yards were flooded, so we had to traverse a narrow walkway whose surface consisted of two logs tied together, about a foot above the dark water.

The villagers, who were used to this, skipped along briskly, but I wobbled several times and was afraid I might fall in. Lynn felt much the same, and when we emerged from the cave she declared, "I'm not going back through there!" But our guide told us that we would have to, as it was the only way back to our village.

Lynn spent the next few hours worrying about the upcoming ordeal. When we returned to the cave and reached the log walkway, she froze. Our guide, incredibly patient, walked backwards in front of her, holding her hands and murmuring that everything would be okay. She trusted the guide, gripped his hands, and made it safely over the dark water. Then he came back and did the same for me.

Now Dr. Hellmann and Frank are the guides, holding Lynn's hands and escorting her to a place of safety. You have to trust your guides.

The kyphoplasty procedures go well; the sharp and dreadful back pain disappears almost immediately. But Lynn's hips still hurt, making walking difficult, and now other things start to go wrong.

In October, Lynn undergoes a needle biopsy of the largest tumor in her pelvis, and then receives an intravenous dose of chemo to hold down the cancer while we wait for the genetic analysis.

The chemo has "mixed" results: Some of the tumors remain stable while others are growing, but none have shrunk. Dr. Hellmann is reluctant to try a stronger cocktail because Lynn has proven to be hypersensitive to every drug she's ever taken. He thinks she won't be able to tolerate the side effects.

Luckily, the genetic analysis identifies a new mutation, which is probably what enabled the tumors to beat the Tagrisso but also gives us several lines of attack. Lynn can either take a new experimental drug designed to destroy tumors like these; or she can continue taking Tagrisso while adding in a second drug that has been shown, in other types of cancer, to attack tumors that have the mutation.

Neither treatment is guaranteed to work, but Dr. Hellmann says, "I don't want to sound like a Pollyanna here, but it seems to me we still have a shot."

It is a difficult choice. The clinical trial is managed by a different oncologist, so choosing it will mean leaving Dr. Hellmann and getting to know an entirely new team. But our success five years ago with immunotherapy gives us reason to hope, and it doesn't hurt that the trial will pay for Lynn's expensive drugs. Also, Dr. Hellmann assures us that he will be kept in the loop and available whenever we need him.

We choose the clinical trial. We say an emotional goodbye to Dr. Hellmann and Maureen, hugging them both, and in late November, I finally write a CaringBridge post, my first in almost three years.

Tuesday, November 24, 2020
www.CaringBridge.org/LynnKotula

Six years ago tomorrow, Lynn received her first treatment for metastasized lung cancer. It worked spectacularly well and held down her cancer for more than five years. Most of the problems she subsequently experienced were caused by damage to her spine, not the cancer itself. Given how deadly lung cancer is, those years qualify as a minor miracle.

Unfortunately, last winter Lynn's cancer mutated again. One of the tumors in her lung began to grow, and there are now multiple tumors in Lynn's spine and pelvic bones, causing great pain.

Three weeks ago we received promising news: A genetic analysis showed that Lynn's new tumors share a mutation, called an MET, that wasn't present in her original tumors, and which is thought to be what enabled the cancer to beat the drugs. More importantly, a new drug is designed to destroy MET-positive tumors. The drug is so new that fewer than a hundred people have taken it thus far.

It's said that history doesn't repeat itself, but it often rhymes, and today it rhymed for Lynn. This morning she received her first infusion of the new drug, which holds the same promise that her immunotherapy did six years ago. If it works, it could potentially have a miraculous effect and kill off Lynn's tumors. Or it might hold them at bay, as the last drugs did, for years. Or it might do nothing.

Over the next few months, we will find out what it does.

Lynn receives several infusions of the experimental drug. It goes smoothly, but we don't warm to the new oncologist. He is more clinical than Dr. Hellmann, more focused on the science and less on us as people. Everything is crisp and efficient, like Sloan's new outpatient building, but we miss the friendly touch of Dr. Hellmann and Maureen, and the corridors lined with interesting artwork.

For two weeks Lynn's back pain steadily worsens until she can barely get out of bed, so Dr. Bilsky orders another set of MRIs. Turns out it's not tumors causing the pain, but rather another collapsed vertebra. Unfortunately, this is also the bone that anchors the two titanium rods in her back. The rods are now angled forward, which explains why, for the past few weeks, Lynn has repeatedly complained that she can't seem to stand up straight.

The only way to fix this is via an operation in which Dr. Bilsky will open Lynn's back, remove the existing rods, and replace them with slightly longer ones. In the four years since the last operation, the technology has advanced, and he is confident that it will eliminate most of her pain. As spinal operations go, "it's not a heavy lift." But it is still a major operation.

It is also elective. Lynn's spinal cord is not in danger, and in theory she could skip the operation and live with the pain. But this is her best chance to get her life back. Again, she overcomes her fear and commits to the procedure.

Lynn hasn't been able to enjoy a walk outside since early November, six weeks ago. Walking, which used to give her so much pleasure, has become too painful. She did go out with my sister, Francie, and her husband over Thanksgiving weekend, when they drove us seven blocks uptown to see a barred owl in Riverside Park, a rare occurrence in our neck of the woods. Luckily, it was sitting on a branch more or less where we expected. I held the binoculars for Lynn because her hands were shaking too much. She got a good look, and then we walked slowly back to our apartment, Lynn with one hand cupped in the crook of my arm and the other on her cane.

Several times after that we managed to meet with friends outdoors. We brought pillows and a folding chair and sat on a park bench just a block from our apartment, enjoying the mild weather.

Then Lynn stopped going out at all, except for the many trips to Sloan.

Friday, December 18, 2020
www.CaringBridge.org/LynnKotula

Lynn is out of surgery and in the recovery room, doing well.

Everything went smoothly. They replaced the broken hardware and extended the rods. Dr. Bilsky cemented the screws into her bone and injected cement into each of her lower-back vertebrae that hadn't already been cemented. As he said, "We used a lot of cement," and he felt this was likely to hold for a long time.

26 comments

So glad to hear the op went well—medical heavy engineering at its best! —Antony

Thank you, Tony, thank you Sloan K. And not to forget—thank you Big Nick's Cement Inc.! —Maria Pia

Lynn's recovery begins well. On Sunday she manages to sit on the edge of her bed and then stand up—twice—without swearing. By Monday she is no longer taking intravenous pain medication and eats reasonably well on her own.

But there is a flip side to this good news: Sloan is starting to plan for Lynn's discharge on either Wednesday or Thursday. Since she will not be able to take care of herself at home, they once again recommend that she transfer to a subacute rehab facility where, they think, a few weeks of intensive physical therapy will get her to "another level."

The problem is that we've seen this movie before, and we didn't like it. So I decide to ignore Sloan's recommendation and bring Lynn home. I spend two days making phone calls to line up PT/OT services and a home health aide for the first few days to help me learn how to take care of her. Sorting this out isn't easy, but I manage to arrange everything in time for her upcoming Wednesday discharge.

On Monday, Lynn is slightly delirious, and it worsens on Tuesday. This freaks me out, as I dread a repeat of what happened before. But the palliative care team thinks it's because her pain level has gone down faster than they can decrease the methadone and will soon pass.

On Tuesday night, Lynn has an episode of atrial fibrillation, so they postpone discharge to Thursday to make sure it is just a blip.

On Wednesday, Lynn continues to have mild cardiac episodes and her delirium worsens. She hides most of this from the staff, only expressing her delusions, paranoia, and fear to me. They have no idea how miserable she is and how desperately she wants to go home.

So, when the charge nurse tells me on Thursday morning that they again want to postpone discharge because of the cardiac issues, I put my foot down. "Lynn is going home today whether you like it or not," I say. "Everything we've done for the past five years has been to help her live life as fully as possible. If she has a heart attack and dies at home, that will be better than losing her mind in the hospital. She already has terminal cancer, for God's sake!"

I get louder and more emphatic with each sentence; by the end of the speech, I am practically shouting. We compromise on a few more hours of observation, and Lynn comes home late that afternoon.

Sunday, December 27, 2020
www.CaringBridge.org/LynnKotula

After three days at home, we are clearly on the right track. All of Lynn's vital signs are good. She cannot get out of bed without help, but once up, she shuffles around the apartment with her walker, and we eat all our meals at the kitchen table. When she is in bed, her favorite cat sleeps on her stomach.

Lynn's head is steadily clearing. Although she has moments of delirium, I am able to tell her that whatever she thinks just happened was in her head, and she quickly comes back to reality. All good, and so much better than when she went to rehab in 2016, and it took three months to get this far.

I am omitting the difficult parts. Home care after spinal surgery is no picnic, though Lynn's daily improvements give me hope. I am typing this post in the first true downtime I've had since Lynn came home.

Lynn keeps making plans to reply to emails or call friends, but her fingers shake too much, and the best intentions turn into afternoon naps. She does read all the emails and answers the phone now and then, and when she does so, she is happy to talk.

29 comments

Sounds like a GREAT choice. I know from multiple hospital rounds with my mom that everything gets orders of magnitude better in familiar surroundings. —Ann

So glad to hear the home delivery was successful. No answering emails allowed. —Laura

IT AIN'T EASY

From late December onward, it is just the two of us alone together in the apartment, except for the few days when we have aides. At first, I am still working, but my hours are flexible and I can work remotely, so I take care of business in the morning and devote the rest of the day to Lynn.

It's amazing how quickly time passes just dealing with the business of living, as well as the business of cancer. Endless speakerphone calls with Lynn's doctors and nurses, frequent appointments involving painful taxi rides, hours spent waiting in various Sloan buildings. Eventually, I take a leave of absence to care for Lynn full-time.

Our shared intimacy is a gift and a burden: We've never felt closer, but the work never stops. I do all the shopping and cooking, and we eat every meal together, sitting at the kitchen table where Lynn has a beautiful view of the Hudson River. I help her get in and out of bed, on and off the commode, and from one room to another in the apartment. I schedule the appointments with the professionals who come to see us. And in the evenings, I wheel Lynn into the living room and help her settle onto the sofa so we can watch TV together.

Lynn and I talk frequently about what is happening in her body, speculating about each new pain, wondering whether they are muscular or an indication that the miracle drug has stopped working. I don't write about this at the time; it is just the ordinary fabric of our life now, albeit repetitive. Not the sort of topic, I think, that would merit a journal entry.

Lynn has physical therapy at home four days in a row, and though she still can't get out of bed without assistance, once upright her shuffling with the walker turns into actual steps, and she is standing straighter than she has in months.

On Wednesday she starts using a rollator instead of the walker, and on Friday we stop having home health aides. By the weekend, she can get in and out of bed by herself, though the process involves a series of grunts and curses that she tells me to ignore. A weight begins to lift from our shoulders, and we start to imagine going to Blairstown next summer.

And that's when I realize that I've been living with a hernia for weeks.

It started last December, when I began to feel a strange, persistent itch on my inner thigh. I examined my skin closely, but there was no rash or bug bite, and I thought that perhaps I needed to try a different laundry detergent.

Later, I noticed that walking from the subway to the hospital was becoming uncomfortable, but I assumed I'd pulled a muscle.

Then one day in January, I'm in the shower, soaping up, when my fingers brush against a bulge in my abdomen, under my pubic hair, that sends an electric shock through my groin. I can't believe it. This hernia has been here all the time, interfering with my nerves and causing the strange itching, but I was so focused on Lynn that I missed it.

Two weeks later, I take a six-hour break from caregiving to have the hernia repaired, an outpatient procedure that requires general anesthesia. While drifting awake and idly scrolling my phone, I notice a Facebook message from a friend about an album he's just released. When I last heard from him, he was celebrating his marriage to his second wife, which took place a few years after the sudden death of his beloved first wife.

Still pleasantly high on anesthesia, I write:

Hi Pat, I happen to be in the recovery room after a hernia repair and yours was the first message I received. Last time I logged into Facebook, you had just put up a post celebrating your new relationship, and I was very pleased to read it. Great that you are solidly into your next chapter.

Lynn has been living with stage IV lung cancer for over six years now. She is still very much with us, so I am not immediately thinking that far ahead, but it is nice to be reminded that second chapters are possible.

Released by the drugs from my normal filters, I've shared a thought that I previously reserved for therapy: That someday, possibly soon, I will have to make a life without

Lynn. Then I bury it as deeply as I can and head home to be at her side.

∽

Lynn insists on helping me as much as possible. She can't stand up for more than a minute, so when there are vegetables to chop, I put the cutting board on the kitchen table and she sits in a chair, slowly slicing through them. When it's time to load the dishwasher, she sits next to it, and I hand her the plates one at a time.

I could do all of these things more quickly, but she insists on sharing the burden, and I am happy to have her company.

Because of COVID, most of our friends are unable to visit, so Lynn spends hours on the phone with them, and between calls she sits at her computer scrolling through Facebook, a smile fixed firmly on her face.

Facebook is extremely important to Lynn. Her friends post photos of their recent paintings, and occasionally she posts a photo of one of her many drawings. They are recreating the artistic community they used to have before the pandemic closed their galleries.

Then new pains start, several of them. At first, we assume this is a result of all the PT, but as the weekend wears on that theory loses credence, and we realize it is probably the bone cancer. The spot in her pelvic bone that hurts most is also the site of her largest tumor.

Early in the month, Lynn has a series of CT scans to see whether the experimental drug is working. When her new oncologist eyeballs them, his impression is that the drug is preventing her tumors from growing. But the radiology reports, which we read a few days later, are sobering. There are three tumors in Lynn's lungs and fifteen or twenty in her bones. Some have shrunk, some are sclerotic—so the experimental drug must be doing something—but there are new tumors in her neck (cervical spine) that weren't there a few weeks ago. Dr. Bilsky says they aren't causing imminent danger, but it is beyond depressing to think that Lynn is fighting so hard to come back from surgery and still has all these tumors.

Each morning when she wakes, Lynn feels good, looks forward to getting out of bed and going to her studio to paint, as if the cancer and the pain were all a bad dream. Then she tries to move and reality kicks in. It is a bittersweet gift: The moment of joy at the start of each day followed by the inevitable sadness.

After three weeks of radio silence while we hoped things would improve, I finally share the news with our friends.

Friday, January 29, 2021
www.CaringBridge.org/LynnKotula

This has been a terrible period, made more so because the operation went smoothly, and Lynn had started to move nicely and do in-home PT. We were crushed when her pain suddenly became debilitating, and it has been difficult to remain optimistic since then. The occasional improvements are so small that we almost don't notice them, and they are followed by obvious setbacks.

Lynn is moving like a ninety-year-old with severe arthritis. Everything is an effort. Everything hurts. She is unable to take over-the-counter pain relievers because of interactions with her other meds, and even tiny doses of muscle relaxants knock her out (it wasn't fun finding that out). Topical anti-inflammatory gel (Voltaren) helps, at least for a few hours in the specific locations where we apply it. We are going through the stuff rather quickly. The physical therapist put Lynn's sessions on hold because they were making things worse. The only solution is to let her muscles heal while gently moving around the house and doing small sets of mild stretches to keep them awake.

Meanwhile, this assault on Lynn's system has slowed her thinking and makes her sleepy. She is still herself, just slower in both motion and speech. Sometimes very slow if she's recently taken a pain med or muscle relaxer. And it is affecting me; I find myself talking, even thinking, at Lynn's speed in order to stay in sync with her. We are slogging through a swamp together.

A few minutes ago, as I tried to get Lynn settled into a chair so she can draw the cats, she turned to me and said, "It ain't easy, Bud."

I know this time will pass, but it ain't easy.

20 comments

Counting one's blessings at a time like this seems absurd. However, one rare and beautiful blessing is that you have each other. —Terry

The weeks before and after that post are full of physical pain and a growing suspicion that this isn't just muscular. But we don't want our friends and family to fear for us; we don't want to indulge in self-pity or pain porn. And, of course, I hope that by not sharing the full truth of our experience, our worst fears will never materialize.

The pain starts in Lynn's thigh, which I do think was caused by overenthusiastic physical therapy. She relished pushing herself through those exercises. The therapist, an optimistic, technically skilled man still early in his career, will later tell her that he learned a lot from working with her. "I shouldn't have listened when you encouraged me to keep going. But your enthusiasm was so compelling! Next time, I will trust my training more."

As Lynn's overstressed thigh recovers, the pain moves upward, into her torso. We call Dr. Bilsky's nurse, Cynthia, and she reassures us that this is normal.

"The surgery interfered with the nerves that wrap around your body," she says. "It's pretty common to experience pain there during recovery." This is reassuring, as it helps us continue to believe that Lynn is healing. Even when she begins thinking and speaking agonizingly slowly, we assume it's because of all the pain and medications, not something worse.

At about that time Lynn starts talking about her eyesight.

Something strange began happening late in the summer when, very occasionally, she would see something surprising out of the corner of her left eye. Several times she thought she saw a plant, a fern (though we don't own any), and at other times one of the cats—or once a shiny white poodle. At first, these were rare occurrences at a time when we were adjusting her pain medications, so we ascribed the visions to her mildly addled brain playing tricks on her. Lynn thought they were puzzling but also rather silly and even pleasant.

By late fall, the visions became more frequent. Lynn began involuntarily closing her left eye while watching TV or trying to read. If I looked at her from that side, I thought she'd fallen asleep. But we were distracted by everything else and never remembered to mention this issue to the oncology team.

Now, it is worse: She no longer enjoys reading or watching TV, and we finally start to consider that these symptoms might be caused by a brain tumor. When Lynn goes for her next infusion, we tell the team about her vision and the growing pain in her upper body as well as other worrying symptoms, such as occasional difficulty holding her sphincter closed.

The team takes these reports seriously. They arrange an emergency MRI to make sure the trouble with Lynn's sphincter isn't the result of spinal cord compression; schedule a visit with Lynn's ophthalmologist, who is also at Sloan; and schedule a brain scan the week after. They tell us there could be many reasons for the vision issues, so they want an eye exam to rule out the more benign ones and a brain scan to check for tumors.

The week before Lynn's eye exam, the pain in her neck worsens, overshadowing everything else. But we still believe, or at least hope, that this is part of the healing process, nerve signals gone awry. The physical therapist comes several times and mildly massages Lynn's back and neck. This soothes her, but the relief doesn't last.

I use a great deal of Voltaren anti-inflammatory gel on Lynn's neck and upper body, probably three or four times the maximum daily dose. We also try CBD oil, but Voltaren provides the best results. Lynn becomes fond of its partic-ular smell, and we both look forward to when I don gloves and spread it on her arms, under her breasts, and up and down her spine.

∽

By the time Lynn has her eye exam, her neck pain is excruciating. The taxi ride doesn't help. Over the previous months, we've become adept at getting Lynn downstairs in her travel wheelchair, transferring her lumbar pillow into the car seat, and then instructing the driver to avoid potholes and drive slowly. This is difficult to do in a New York winter, but virtually every driver does their best, letting other traffic pass by and inching over any potholes. Still, Lynn frequently gasps or cries out when we hit an unavoidable bump.

This morning we have bad luck: The springs in the cab are shot, the seat worn, and the driver doesn't seem to hear as we repeatedly ask him to be more careful. Lynn is jostled again and again, and when we arrive at the eye doctor's office, her neck is throbbing. I have to give her extra pain meds to make it through the exam.

Worse, before Lynn can see Dr. Francis, the technicians insist on doing those eye tests where you have to place your chin on a cup-like ledge and press your forehead against a bar, which triggers a searing stab of pain.

Lynn manages to do all of the tests. Repeatedly, she feels pain and backs away, saying, "No, I can't," but after a moment she leans forward again and works with the technician to find a way to get it done.

Lynn's left eye is much worse than her right. When the technician asks her to read a row of letters with her left eye, Lynn says, "Which one?" because she sees two rows of letters on the screen when there is only one.

By the time Dr. Francis arrives, Lynn is a wreck. We tell her what happened, and she swings her usual equipment out of the way and uses a hand-held light to peer into Lynn's eyes.

"The good news," she announces, "is that there's no sign of cancer in your eyes." But that is not the end of the story. "Everything you've been talking about, the oddities in your peripheral vision, the closed left eye, are symptoms of double vision. That's not necessarily because of a tumor; there can be many causes, but a tumor is a real possibility." We tell Dr. Francis about the upcoming brain scan, and she says she will add a scan of Lynn's eye sockets as well.

"If you want help with the double vision," says Dr. Francis, "we can fit you for prism glasses. But not today because your eyes are already dilated."

Lynn shakes her head, she just wants to go home. But at breakfast the next morning she reconsiders and decides she would like to be able to read again. We are still trying to believe that there will be time for that.

Over the next few days, Lynn loses the ability to hold up her head. She walks around with it stuck straight out in front, looking down at the floor.

Lynn hates this, keeps trying to pull it back up, but a few minutes later, it is down again. She also starts experiencing a shooting pain down her left arm and into her hand, which seems to come and go randomly. On Friday, the physical therapist puts the two together. "When your head is down, it pinches the nerves that run down your left arm. If you are able to hold it up, or you lie on your back with your neck supported, the arm pain goes away."

You'd think we would have called Dr. Bilsky's office right away, but it takes us a couple of days to get around to it. Lynn keeps living with these increasing levels of pain and physical indignities, hoping they are a natural part of her recovery.

But it is getting harder and harder to hold onto that illusion, so over the weekend we email nurse Cynthia about Lynn's symptoms, and on Monday she replies that the description of Lynn's neck pain is extremely significant. She arranges for an MRI of Lynn's cervical spine the following morning, when Lynn is already scheduled for her second COVID shot.

Tuesday is another excruciating day. The MRI is scheduled for 9:30 a.m., so we arrive at 9:00, which requires waking up at 6:30 because it takes Lynn forever to pull herself together, eat a few bites of food, and leave the house. Once at Sloan, we have to negotiate getting Lynn out of her wheelchair and into the hospital gown, all of which is done at a snail's pace to minimize her pain. It takes three people to get Lynn safely up on the table for the scan, and to help her down again afterwards.

Then it is 12:30 p.m. and time to meet with Dr. Bilsky and Cynthia to discuss the scan. Although it has not yet been read by a radiologist, Dr. Bilsky can see that Lynn has two broken vertebrae in her neck, which I guess is not a total surprise.

Dr. Bilsky says there are two possible ways to eliminate the pain: Have another major operation, which doesn't sound good to any of us, or wear a neck brace for at least six weeks. "The brace will give the vertebrae a chance to heal in a reasonably appropriate position," he says. "After six weeks we can try taking it off. If all goes well, you should be able to hold your head up without pain."

Given this lousy choice, Lynn opts for the brace. Cynthia calls an office in the nearby Hospital for Special Surgery and tells us that if we go over there right away, Lynn can be fitted for a brace that afternoon.

After lunch and Lynn's COVID shot, we set out to get her neck brace, six blocks away. It is raining lightly and there are no cabs in sight. I figure that the process of getting Lynn in and out of a taxi will cause more pain, so I push her the six blocks. Now, I am the taxi driver, trying to avoid every bump on the sidewalks, but I can't do it any better than those professional drivers. Lynn keeps sucking in her teeth and crying out; it is yet another ordeal for both of us.

When we arrive at the HSS waiting room, an assistant brings over some forms that Lynn needs to sign so Medicare will pay for the brace.

Lynn pushes them away. "No," she says. "Leave me alone." She no longer understands why she needs a brace or remembers the discussions we had with Cynthia and Dr. Bilsky just two hours earlier.

"It hurts," she says, again and again. "I want to go home."

I plead with Lynn to sign the forms. "This is the only way to make the pain go away. It's why I pushed you all the way here. Please, just sign. Then we can go home."

Eventually she gives in, I think more because she wants to make me happy than because she understands or agrees.

An hour later Lynn is wearing her new neck brace, and we head home in a taxi. But in the cab she keeps trying to take it off, and I keep having to explain that she needs to wear it for the next few weeks, that this is how we will stop the pain. We are still having a version of that argument when we arrive home.

Before we can even take off our coats, Lynn's cell phone rings. It is Cynthia calling to tell us that she has Lynn's MRI report and there is more bad news: There are new tumors in Lynn's spine, neck, and lower brain that need to be addressed. "The spinal team has discussed your case," she says. "They recommend you be admitted to the hospital first thing tomorrow to start a course of radiation. Even waiting three days for your scheduled brain scan will be too long."

Lynn, who has been speaking fuzzily after such a long and painful day, suddenly becomes clear. "I'm not going to the hospital tomorrow," she says. "I can't go back to the hospital. I want to be home for at least two nights."

"Of course, that's your choice," says Cynthia. "We can always start radiation on Thursday. I'll arrange a bed for you." I can hear the disappointment in her voice.

Lynn and I wonder what to do. It is so seductive: The team is offering a next step that might buy us much-needed time.

She asks me what I think.

"I don't know," I say. "Part of me wants you to do it. Maybe the radiation can slow down the tumors and give the drugs a chance to work. But it's all getting so hard. What if you go in for just a couple of days and then come home after that?" I'm caught up in the momentum, advocating exactly the kind of last-ditch treatment that I always hoped to avoid.

For a few minutes, we consider this choice. Lynn clearly thinks it is a bad idea to go to the hospital, but her words come slowly. She seems more afraid of my disappointment than of what stopping treatment would mean for her.

Then the phone rings, and it is Dr. Hellmann telling us exactly what we need to hear.

Tuesday, February 9, 2021
www.CaringBridge.org/LynnKotula

We learned today that the reason Lynn has been in such pain is that another vertebra has fractured—this time in her neck. And there are now lesions in her brain.

Dr. Bilsky and the radiation oncologists proposed that Lynn check back into the hospital to start a course of radiation. Lynn hated the idea, and we were wrestling with the implications when the phone rang. It was Dr. Hellmann, our beloved oncologist, whom we have greatly missed since Lynn went into the clinical trial last fall.

Dr. Hellmann said he had just read the reports. The cancer in Lynn's spine and pelvis has become much worse and is now visible in Lynn's lower brain. Just four months ago, it was Dr. Hellmann who encouraged us not to give up hope, who said we still have a chance to beat this thing for a few more years. Now, he gently suggested that perhaps the time has come to stop treatment. Perhaps it is time to stop trying to fix each problem when the treatments themselves are starting to feel like torture, and instead focus on staying home and being comfortable. In his words, "Sometimes you have to say enough is enough."

In short, home hospice care.

It is time. Dr. Hellmann said we should expect to have weeks, not months, left together. Lynn and I are just starting to process this, but it is not really a surprise, and in many ways should be a relief compared to these past few months.

I write the post quickly and upload it to CaringBridge. Within hours there are dozens of responses from our dear, dear friends.

32 Comments

Your courage over the past few months has been truly amazing. Sending you much love. —Sue and Arthur

I am at a loss for words & holding you both in my heart. May this ultimately bring you great peace. Always truly, madly, deeply. —Libby

I think we all read your words "our beloved oncologist" and real-ize how deeply, deeply considered this moment is. Of course (!) we should all choose comfort over anything that feels "like torture." Comfort is the very least you both deserve. —David

TRAVELING

"Sometimes you have to say enough is enough."

It is late afternoon. Lynn and I are in the living room, she in her wheelchair, me in a folding chair in front of her. There is one light on, leaving most of the room in shadow.

Dr. Hellmann speaks calmly, gently. "If you go back to the hospital now, you will probably never come out," he says. "The radiation may slow it a little, but there's just too much cancer. We're not going to beat it, and the treatments will make you even weaker. If there's ever a time to stop treatment, this is it."

Lynn lets out a long sigh, her eyes brimming. Then she nods and says, "Yes, I'm ready. Let's stop." Her voice is thick, the words come slowly, and for the first time I acknowledge that it's not just the pain that is doing this to her but also the tumors in her brain.

Part of me can't believe all our work is over. And yet, it is also a relief. Ever since the cancer began growing again, we've been winding a spring tighter and tighter, each turn more difficult than the last, until finally even one more twist is beyond our strength. Now, we can let go and just be together.

Dr. Hellmann says he will put in the order for home hospice; we should expect to hear from a social worker in the morning. Lynn asks whether we need to tell Cynthia that she's not coming in for radiation, and Dr. Hellmann says no, he will take care of it.

We hang up and sit quietly for a minute, then I go into the office and write the post to tell our friends. When it's done, I heat up a light dinner, and for the third time Lynn and I sit at the small kitchen table holding hands and talking about what's truly important. We did this seven years ago, after the initial phone call from Dr. Weinstein, and then again when we came back to the city last fall and had to start treatment all over again. Now I think we both know that this is the last time we will get to talk like this.

Lynn is still in her wheelchair, clearly experiencing intense pain. She speaks haltingly, in short sentences, as we try to give each other comfort.

We imagine how hospice will play out, what dying will feel like, how I will be afterward, and what I will do. I promise Lynn that, to the extent possible in a state where assisted suicide is against the law, she will have control over her death. All she has to do is stop eating and drinking and the end will come fairly soon. "No matter what happens, I will never force food or liquid into your mouth. If you close your lips, I will understand what that means."

It is the most important promise I have ever made.

Then it's Lynn's turn to say a series of sentences that I don't interrupt. We are talking about what will happen after she's gone, when suddenly she says: "I want you to get another girlfriend." Then she pauses and shakes her head: "No, I don't want you to have a girlfriend." Then:

"I do want you to have a girlfriend." Then: "No, I don't ever want you to have a girlfriend." And finally, after a longer pause and a more forceful nod, "I want you to have a girlfriend."

Lynn wants to keep living but knows she can't; she wants to hold on to me and the cats forever but knows she can't, and she wants to take care of me as much as I want to take care of her. She wants to give me the comfort of another happy life, another girlfriend, and she also wants me to stay bound to her forever. And she is comfortable enough with the contradiction to let me know both.

Wednesday, February 10, 2021

Lynn is leaving us faster than I expected.

Overnight she sleeps soundly. She seems to be at peace, and we fall asleep holding hands. But when morning comes, she has trouble getting out of bed, for it is so very painful. She only eats a few bites of breakfast and then returns to bed, where she spends the day alternately snoozing and lost in thought.

I spend the day dealing with logistics and arranging for friends to visit. Six people from the hospice service and the nursing agency come for intake appointments; the social worker and a nurse will be here tomorrow, the aide will start on Friday. There is a lot of information and paperwork, and our quiet apartment is suddenly full of strangers.

After they leave, I sit for a while in the bedroom watching Lynn sleep, wondering whether we will ever be able to talk again as we did last night. Then I publish a post on CaringBridge and am flooded with supportive comments.

Tony, I am so sorry. I love Lynn, too, and would just wish her a life without pain. —Jane

Would that love were enough. It is not. But in the end, it's all we really have. Fill the time you have with it. —Dave

The next day, Lynn is much more present and alert, and starts having second thoughts about hospice. At breakfast she wonders whether there is a chance we could resume treatment and gain more time. I download the full MRI report and she has me read it to her, every word, as we sit together in the morning light.

The report is devastating. The cancer has infiltrated Lynn's entire spine and pelvis. It is no longer described in terms of discrete tumors, but rather as if it were a fluid flowing in and around her spinal and pelvic bones, and of course it is also visible in her brain. This is what Dr. Hellmann saw when he suggested that the time had come to stop treatment.

Lynn listens closely as I read the report. Her eyes grow sad, but she does not speak.

Thursday, February 11, 2021
www.CaringBridge.org/LynnKotula

Throughout Lynn's treatment, she never felt brave; she just kept looking at the options and taking whatever step seemed best. But she was very afraid of pain. She often said that while she didn't fear dying, she didn't want to be in pain, and she was terribly afraid that anesthesia would trigger another bout of delirium.

So when Lynn decided to have several more kyphoplasties in October 2020 and a third major spinal surgery

two months later, she was being very brave. She over-
came her worst fears to take the next step toward what
we hoped would be a few more good years. But when the
drugs stopped working and she decided to start hospice,
it wasn't bravery but rather an acknowledgment that her
path had narrowed and there were no more steps to take.

Two good days in a row now, though the pattern is different today. Lynn has several hours of energy in the morning, then crashes until a second wind lifts her in late afternoon, when she manages a video call with a dear friend
who is in Japan this week. It is tearful and joyous and gives
Lynn a strong tailwind that lasts through a lovely conversation over dinner. She drifts off to sleep comfortably, as
if nothing special were happening.

Friday, February 12, 2021
www.CaringBridge.org/LynnKotula

I am getting hospice services in place and feel incredibly
supported both by your comments and by the professionals who are coming into the house. There are tough
times ahead, but I hope we will have a nice stretch here.
Whether for days or weeks, who knows?

I don't plan to keep posting every day like this, but so
many friends wished for a series of good days that I
wanted to let you all know that this has happened. The
nights are usually hardest (and very intimate and special,
as I've said), so we'll see if the good day stretches all the
way to dawn, but at least we know this is possible.

I keep meaning to say, and perhaps already have, that
whether animated or fast asleep, Lynn is much more at

peace now than during the last six months. We are able to talk with clarity and serenity about the decision, what lies ahead, and what is happening to her now. This, too, will pass as the brain tumors do their damage, but we are starting out in a very good place.

All day long Lynn worries that we are working the aides too hard, that they won't have enough time to get home, and that we haven't done a good enough job offering beverages or snacks to visitors.

She wants to eat and says she enjoys the food, but she takes only a few bites of each dish over a period of several hours. Then she sleeps eleven hours overnight. There is little time left when she is able to be alert or interact with friends. She has even stopped drawing the cats.

The social worker tells me that people in hospice often reach a point where they completely stop eating and drinking. Lynn is not at that point, possibly nowhere near. The problem is those brain tumors, which are stealing her from us as she develops a form of dementia at a fast pace.

Saturday, February 13, 2021
www.CaringBridge.org/LynnKotula

Lynn is increasingly having trouble finding the right words. If she or someone else happens to use a word— say "carrot," for example—a moment later she may say something like, "I need to use the carrot," when she means "toilet." She knows what she wants to say but assembles the sentence from whatever words she can access at that moment. She realizes it's not the right word, but she wants so much to express the thought that she says it however she can.

When Lynn has energy, she can stand up from her wheel-chair, turn, and sit down on the commode; it's relatively straightforward. But when her brain is tired, she forgets how to do these things, and I can spend five minutes say-ing, "come this way" and "just a little more" and then, "No, THIS way, towards me, slide your feet," and it takes a lot longer. She absolutely insists on doing all this her-self. She still has her pride and does not want help.

Overnight, things are simpler, as I have found a female urinal that I can hold against her, so she does not have to get out of bed. Tonight we switched to adult diapers, and she said, "Oh good!" and enjoyed putting one on. A few weeks ago, she hated the idea.

When I see photos of Lynn taken during this period, I am surprised by how old she looks. Living with her day-to-day, I've barely noticed the changes, but the cancer, pain, and powerful drugs have accelerated the aging process. She looks twenty years older than just twelve months ago.

When I first met Lynn, I worried about our ten-year age difference; that as she aged, there would come a time when I would feel like I was married to an old lady, and this scared me. My father was more than twenty years older than my mother, and when he entered his seven-ties, he pulled away from her, began looking and acting more like her father rather than her husband. Their rela-tionship deteriorated, and they moved apart. I was suf-ficiently affected by this that when I realized I was fall-ing for Lynn, I promptly broke up with her, told her that I couldn't love someone that much older than me. Then I missed her so much that I came crawling back just a few days later, begging for forgiveness. She was furious; I had deeply hurt her, but she agreed to accept me if I never said anything like that again.

For most of our marriage, the age difference didn't matter; Lynn always looked and acted at least ten years younger than she was. But now she looks like my mother, or perhaps my grandmother, and I make a wonderful discovery: It still doesn't matter. The Lynn I fell in love with is very much present even as her body fails: her spirit, her laugh, the twinkle in her eye. I don't see her the way the camera does. I see Lynn as I have always known her: young at heart and full of life.

Sunday, February 14, 2021

It is a privilege and a pleasure to lie in bed at night and hold Lynn's hand and listen to her breathe. Her broken neck is a dreadful complication in what would otherwise be a more straightforward transition, but we are blessed that when lying in bed she is not in pain and can sleep deeply.

We both love it when she has to pee, and I hold the urinal against her. She lies on her back with her left knee up and I lean my head against it, breathing her scent and gently stroking her calf, while we wait a long time for her to finish. Part of me wishes it would go on forever.

She goes to bed earlier and earlier—8 p.m. tonight—and insists that I come to bed as soon as possible to keep her company, which I do. But I find myself waking and writing posts at 3:00 a.m., rambling on in my night thoughts. That is what it feels like here, now. We are in an intense bubble together, not just at night but all day long. We do not play the radio or read the newspaper; I've barely followed the headlines over the past few weeks; and the aide is very discrete. It's just us together.

Monday, February 15, 2021
www.CaringBridge.org/LynnKotula

Yesterday Lynn had a lovely visit with two friends who braved COVID to drive in and see her, but then afterwards she crashed for several hours. Although she was up later and even called someone at dinnertime, it was clear that her energy store is limited. As I got her into bed, she spoke in monosyllables and told me that having so many interactions was too much and that we need to slow down. So I canceled a few things that had been planned for today in order to make more time for phone calls with friends. Then she slept all afternoon with Lily curled on her chest.

I am back to thinking that Lynn will leave us fairly quickly, at least in the sense of being able to communicate. Her body may live on for a while longer.

I again want to thank all of our amazing friends. Our refrigerator and freezer are overflowing, and if I need something brought to us, there are people right in this building who are happy to help. But more importantly, you have given both Lynn and me the most wonderful gift, which is the ability to have Lynn's memorial while she is able to appreciate it. I always joked, when we went to a good memorial (and aren't most of them good, all those stories and shared emotions) that it was a shame the deceased person wasn't there to appreciate it. Well, guess what, that's what you have given Lynn!

When her energy is low, Lynn only lets me read her two or three messages at a time. Even hearing a friend say, "Sorry I missed you; I'll call back some other time," brings a beautiful smile to her face. I hope everyone who wants to reach Lynn has a chance to do so, but please be aware of the rich experience she is having, even if you are not able to get through.

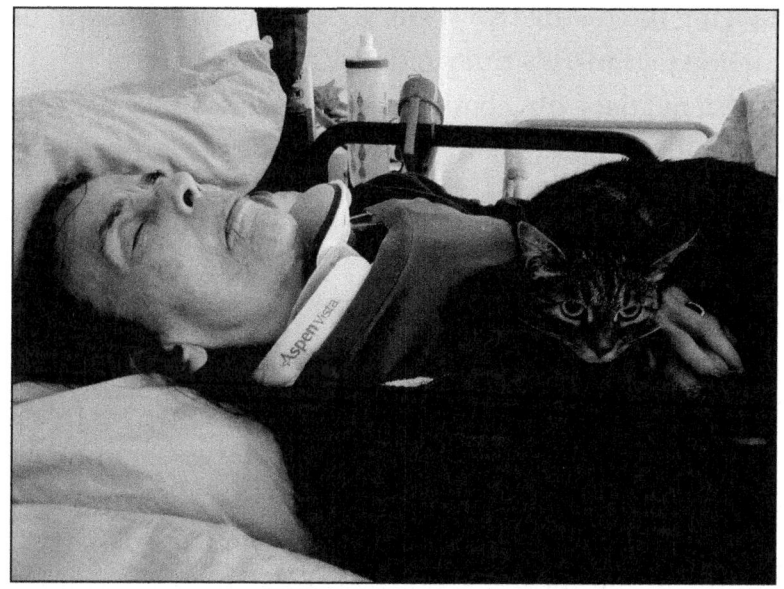

Lynn with Lily, February 15, 2021

The fractures in Lynn's neck are healing. She's worn the cervical collar for a week, and I can see the improvement already: less difficulty getting out of bed, fewer requests for breakthrough pain meds, and no recent episodes of severe debilitating pain.

There is an aide with us from 8 AM to 6 p.m. every day, and not only are they wonderful with Lynn, but they even clean the apartment—really well! And wash the dishes and do the laundry. Until now, our apartment was only this clean when we were preparing to have dinner guests or throw the rare party, and of course it began falling apart as soon as the first guest crossed the threshold. What a treat to spend the day walking on smooth floors, enjoying the distinctive scent of Murphy's Oil Soap. I am starting to think it's time to throw another party.

When I tell Lynn about the party, she says she likes the idea, but she's pretty sure our guests would feel too guilty to have a good time.

Wednesday, February 17, 2021
www.CaringBridge.org/LynnKotula

Between 5 and 7 a.m. this morning, something changed. Lynn was up at 5 and worked with me to use the female urinal: no muss, little fuss. She woke up again an hour later and said she needed to go again, but she couldn't remember how to use the urinal. She insisted on going through the torturous process of standing and transferring to her bedside commode, where she sat for a moment doing nothing, and then I had to help her back to bed. Then, at 7 a.m., she awoke, saying she wanted to pee again, so I suggested she do it in her diaper to avoid having to move. But despite my efforts, she couldn't understand what that meant. I offered her the 7 a.m. pain meds and she refused, saying she hates them. She lay there for a while, then drifted back to sleep.

An aide arrived at 8 a.m. and has made many gentle offers to help Lynn. I believe she managed to change Lynn's diaper. Since then, Lynn has been lying on her back, mostly sleeping. She called for me, and when I came, she asked what I had been up to while away from her. Those were her last spoken words today. She can hear me, but she does not have the energy to respond, other than a small head nod or partial smile.

I told her I was having breakfast, and then started crying. "This is exactly what we hoped for," I said. "That you become increasingly tired until there is no point in talking, then drift off to sleep peacefully." She nodded and smiled.

I am not saying that today is the last day Lynn will be able to speak, but she's experiencing a deeper level of fatigue. If she fully goes to sleep, we will stop feeding her and let nature take its course. If she wakes up hungry, we will give her whatever she asks for but will probably have to shift to soups and smoothies soon.

I called the agency and asked to add overnight coverage, though they're not sure they can get someone here by tonight. I'll be okay in any case, but a second set of hands will make it easier.

The next day, Lynn's energy waxes and wanes unpredictably. She has several good phone conversations in the morning and perks up when a neighbor visits, but then she sleeps all afternoon and doesn't even want me to read aloud her texts from friends.

In the morning she says, out of nowhere, "I don't want to leave yet," and she is still eating small bites of food and drinking sips of milk and smoothies, but each day she has noticeably less energy than the day before. I think she is now sleeping more than eighteen hours a day.

Thursday, February 18, 2021
www.CaringBridge.org/LynnKotula

Dinner brought another sea change: For the first time, Lynn decided to eat in bed. Until today, she cooperated in my efforts to give her at least some vestige of a "normal" life, if only to take her meals in the kitchen and enjoy her favorite view. She's now given up on that view. She has to know that this is the beginning of her end.

Lynn ate tiny bites of soft food (quiche, fish, egg) while propped halfway up against a pile of pillows; it took ten minutes of verbal and physical negotiation to coax her into that position. After dinner we tried to get her under the covers, but she refused to stand up to let us pull them back. "I'm afraid, I'm afraid," she mumbled repeatedly, even though she had stood to use the commode just a few hours ago. At first, I thought she feared the jolt of pain from standing up, but then I wondered if she may also, finally, be afraid of dying.

An aide did come last night, and she was immensely helpful. She sat in a chair at the foot of our bed and handled all the overnight toileting issues while I lay beside Lynn, murmuring encouragement and holding her hand. Since I was no longer responsible for making everything work, I was more relaxed and could quickly fall back asleep even with a third person in the room; hence, no 3 a.m. CaringBridge post. Having these aides should make me less of a midnight writer—and a whole lot calmer.

17 comments

I don't know if you realize how comforting it is for us to have a sense of how Lynn is doing. It's a great gift. —Elizabeth and Mark

Caring for Lynn is a big job now—plenty big enough for two people at a time. This gives you more space to be there as Lynn's husband and partner, as well as her caregiver. —Naomi

Lynn lies on her back breathing smoothly and seems content. But what is she thinking, knowing that her body is betraying her and can no longer get her out of bed? For a woman who prized walking, who still wakes each morning thinking she feels terrific and could jump up and go to her studio, this is a great betrayal.

Friday, February 19, 2021
www.CaringBridge.org/LynnKotula

Lynn is only in pain when she changes position, and now that she can no longer get out of bed, she's decided not to take the breakthrough pain meds. She prefers mental clarity over comfort—and wants to be able to talk to me.

This morning, when she realized I was awake beside her, she said, "I can't believe this is really happening."

"I know," I replied. "Your thoughts are clear, your leg is warm and firm, and we're able to talk to each other. It's impossible to believe that you're about to die. How could this end?"

Then she fell asleep while I was in the middle of a sentence.

∽

Lynn is clear-headed this morning, which is a gift to me. We talk a lot from 5:30 a.m. onward, though early on she says she is feeling too much pain, so I give her an extra pain med crushed in a spoonful of apple sauce. This is the first time she's asked for one in several days. Then an hour later, she asks for another.

While I am eating breakfast, the aide comes to tell me that Lynn says she is going to miss me and miss the cats, so I go in to see her. In a barely audible voice, she says she doesn't want to feel the pain any more. I lean in close to hear her. "I want more methadone," she says.

For six years Lynn has chosen to take less pain medication, accepting moments of pain as the price of clarity in order to participate more fully in her life. Now she wants to leave clarity behind, even though this also means leaving me, her friends, and the cats. She has a greater need to be at peace.

I get in bed and we hold hands under the covers, our heads close together. We have a long conversation about how we think this will play out for her and for me. Lynn has little energy for speaking and communicates mostly with small gestures, using words sparingly. She wants to hear me talk.

"I think, I hope, that you will simply get more and more tired, have nicer and nicer dreams, and slowly drift into them," I say.

"And you?" she asks.

I start crying. I am crying now while typing, the memory is so vivid.

"I'm sure I will go through a period of great grief," I say. "Unbelievable grief. I will miss you terribly. But eventually I'll come out the other side. It may take a year or two, but I'll be okay."

I think we both need to hear this.

Then, with her blessing (and having previously discussed this with the hospice nurse), I give Lynn another methadone, increasing her daily dose from three to four, and she drifts back to sleep.

Methadone is slow to take effect, and this is only a 33 percent increase over Lynn's previous dose—not at all an end-of-life morphine drip. But it is the first step towards that. The clear moments will come less frequently, the pleasant dreams more so.

What a blessing it is to have had these conversations, this experience, together. At least I only have my grief to deal with, not all the other baggage that comes when a life ends too soon.

Sunday, February 21, 2021
www.CaringBridge.org/LynnKotula

We are settling in for what feels like a long voyage in our own private vessel, the two of us going someplace special, though I know it could last as little as a week.

It is quiet here, hushed and intimate. Overnight Lynn becomes disconnected from reality, sometimes fights me and the aide when we try to help her, and last night repeatedly called me "Kirk," which is her brother's name. This is neither uncommon nor unexpected, but that doesn't make it easier.

As the day dawns, she usually starts becoming herself again. This morning, though, she was murmuring nonsense syllables over and over, either to herself or to me, I wasn't sure. I spoke to her anyway, told her about friends who are putting together an online retrospective of her art. Lynn listened, stopped murmuring, and slowly but clearly said: "I don't want a hagiography." Then a moment later: "Don't make a big deal. It's not a big deal." Then she went back to muttering.

For the rest of the morning Lynn barely said anything that made sense, and I thought today would be the day she stops talking. Then a friend came by, and she started chatting, slowly and with lots of pauses but still a small conversation. Then other friends called and several more dropped by; it was the most interactions she'd had in days. She spoke a little with each one, though sometimes she asked me to talk with them in front of her, so she could listen without needing to speak. She was exhausted after each conversation and took many naps. Each sentence she speaks or listens to, comes at a cost.

Lynn no longer gets out of bed; she takes all her meals there. And now a sharp pain in her side kicks in whenever she tries to shift position. She thinks it may be another broken rib, though I suspect it's muscle pain. As most of you know, the cancer has so weakened her bones that she fractured several vertebrae and ribs spontaneously over the past year. I'd hoped that once her neck healed, we'd be past all that. No such luck.

And yet . . .

Lynn continues to eat tiny bites of soft food and sips of smoothies. Her nighttime breathing is regular and strong. Her bladder and bowels work well. She continues to share small meaningful moments with me. She is still here.

On Monday, Lynn speaks only when asked to take a spoonful of medication or a bite of custard or to cooperate with (or refuse) our efforts to keep her clean and dry. Two visitors come and go without getting to see her eyes.

In the morning, she appears to enjoy eating a bite of custard and taking a small sip of smoothie, but a few hours later, when I offer them again, she waves me off.

At about 6 p.m., I give Lynn her evening dose of medication: two pills crushed into a small spoonful of applesauce. She grudgingly allows me to interrupt her nap and drop the applesauce into her mouth, then starts masticating, a process that can take many minutes. I begin to ask if she would like a squirt of water to chase it down, but she interrupts me and says her first two consecutive sentences of the day: "Leave me alone. I've got a lot to do." Then she closes her eyes to get on with doing it.

This is the first time Lynn has refused a voluntary sip of water. She has a lot to do, I think, because she has decided it is time to die.

"Oh! Tony. What a day," writes Anne on CaringBridge. "I would love to know where and what she is working on."

Naomi responds with a story:

I'm reminded that when my mother was at a point akin to where Lynn is now, one of her former aides—a wonderful lady from the West Indies—came to visit and observed "She's traveling." I had never heard the word "traveling" used that way before, but it had meaning for me. I wonder if Lynn's having a lot to do is because she's traveling.

"It sounds like Lynn's spirit is there as she wends her way through the journey," says Sarah.

And from Elizabeth: "It sounds lonely for you."

Tuesday, February 23, 2021
www.CaringBridge.org/LynnKotula

Lynn continues to turn inward, eating and drinking even less (almost nothing today) and talking only when we try to move or feed her. She reminds me of my father and brother, and her father, when we sat with them in hospitals during the last days of their lives. She still rouses from her dreams and tries to help us when we ask her to shift her weight or roll onto her side (which is very painful), but I doubt there will be more moments when she perks up and talks. Now, even a couple of words are enough to surprise and please me.

I think Lynn is aware of my presence, takes comfort from me, hears my words, and knows that she is loved. She no longer listens to text messages; they distract her from where she needs to be. She is no longer able to give much back in the way of clear responses. But what she does give me, when she touches me or tries to speak to me, is all the more meaningful because those moments are so rare.

Lynn has said things to me, small fragments, that make it clear she knows what I am going through. I can't squeeze or hug her; she is too fragile for that, but I did lie beside her this afternoon with my arm lightly across her stomach. When she didn't push my arm away, I started crying, and she touched me and said "Pussycat," followed by a mumbled reassuring half-phrase that I couldn't quite catch. At that moment, I couldn't have felt closer.

After watching Lynn struggle to swallow her midday meds in applesauce, we switched to dissolving them in water and squirted her 5 p.m. meds into her mouth. She fully cooperated by opening her mouth like a baby bird; she even allowed us to give her a squirt of water as a chaser. But that's all she will accept: no further squirts of water, no smoothies, or spoonfuls of custard. She says "She doesn't want it" and keeps her mouth closed when we offer food. She often refers to herself in the third person now, just as she calls the aide "ladies," as in "Stand back, ladies," or "Stop, ladies, stop." Mostly, now, she says "stop" to everything.

Although our friend Elizabeth wrote that "it sounds lonely for you," I don't feel lonely at all. I feel Lynn here; she *is* here. I can hear her breathing in the other room as I type these words. Now that friends have largely stopped visiting and I no longer read texts or emails to Lynn, I relish the silence, the sense that it is just the two of us. In fact, we are only alone for two hours a day; the rest of the time we have company, though they are quite discreet. An aide sits in a chair with us overnight to assist Lynn when she is restless or repeatedly (often erroneously) says she needs to pee, while I sleep surprisingly well beside her.

Our world has been narrowing for six years, year after year. Each time it narrowed, we adjusted to the new normal. No more travel? That's okay, we did so much of that when we could—and Lynn could still paint and we still had each other. No longer able to paint? That's okay, Lynn could draw the cats, and we still had each other.

These past weeks have felt like an acceleration of that process. For the moment it's still okay; we've lost almost everything else that we loved to do, but we still have each other. I will be shattered when Lynn's breathing stops and the apartment is truly empty, but I'm not worrying about that now. We still have each other.

21 comments

You and Lynn are still forming your beautiful, treasured present. —Pam

My sister & I cherished the last days with our mom & felt that somehow we were seeing her out of the world the same way she had seen us into it. —Libby

When you speak of being shattered when Lynn is truly gone, the thing I think is this: Yes, of course, you will be shattered, and you will have to sit with that for a good long while, and it will be so very difficult. But over time, you will take those shattered pieces and build them into a new and beautiful mosaic, and Lynn and the life you have had together will infuse that mosaic. My heart hurts thinking of your loss, but my heart is full thinking of what you will be able to carry forward. —Ann

Lynn is sleeping now, breathing deeply, nothing more. She responds to external stimuli only when we move her, and then only with incoherent mumbles. Yesterday's interaction, when she touched me and called me "Pussycat," could not happen today.

Lynn's last spoken word was "No" after I asked her, early this morning, if she would like a sip of water. It was also the last time she looked at me. Most of the time her eyes are either closed, or she looks upward, unfocused. She seems to have lost the ability to swallow, even by reflex. We are giving only palliative medications, which we dissolve in water and squirt into the hollow of her cheek. She does not acknowledge when we do this, does not respond to the touch of the pipette in her cheek.

But Lynn is present enough to know, when we need to roll her onto her side to change her diaper, that this is for her benefit. While the aide crouches on Lynn's side of the bed, I lie in the middle and pull her shoulder towards me so that she is on her side facing me. She cooperates, using the last of her strength; I then hold her in that position, my right arm pressed firmly against her back to keep her from slipping down.

A few days ago, before we increased the pain medication, this same maneuver caused her extreme pain. She said, "Stop, stop, stop" and "It hurts" over and over; it tormented me to hold her that way. But now that Lynn is no longer in pain, it has become a gentle and intimate maneuver. We do it several times today; one of them is the last time I will hold her.

Wednesday, February 24, 2021
www.CaringBridge.org/LynnKotula

The social worker came to see Lynn and speak with me. He told me that our household is unusual in handling this situation so well, needing little assistance from the hospice team.

One of our aides said something similar about how rare it is to work in a home like ours. When she does hospice duty, the husband (and she did say "husband") often can't cope with the situation and abandons his wife to the aide, unable to talk with her or even acknowledge what is happening. I am happy to be told that I am doing an unusually good job, but also sad for the families for whom this event is traumatic. I think this process is an essential step towards my healing, and a profound journey for Lynn.

Lynn's coloring is still good, her breathing even. The only way we know for certain that she has entered the final phase is her inability to swallow any food or liquids. The social worker says she could die in as little as two or three days, or she could hang on, even without water, for a week or more. I hope Lynn lets go sooner. I think we are both ready.

For the first time since we started hospice, the aide and I are bored. Lynn no longer calls out to us, so we no longer have to drop everything to see what she needs. But the sun is streaming in, the bedroom is bathed in a golden glow, and somehow I'm still not lonely. I settle on the bed beside her and read the paper.

Late in the afternoon, I realize that Lynn is trying to speak to me. I lean in close and ask her to repeat what she said, but her voice is less than a whisper and I am not sure she is using real words. I tell her I'm sorry, but I can't understand her. She shakes her head as if to say there's no point trying to speak; she's moved past words.

It's getting dark, so I turn on a few lights and climb back onto the bed. Lynn's breathing becomes labored, her eyes wide open but unfocused. I notice a few small teardrops on her cheeks. As I wipe them away, I wonder whether they're an automatic secretion or reflect real sadness. I stroke her hair and whisper, "It's all right, you can go; I love you, just let go" over and over as her breathing eases and the moment passes. But I still can't believe her time has come.

Then, without realizing it, I give Lynn the last two conversations she will hear in this life. It is approaching 7:00 p.m., the end of the shift for our daytime aide, Juleika, who has been sitting quietly in a chair at the foot of the bed. Juleika is waiting to check Lynn's diaper one last time before she leaves. The overnight aide isn't due until 9:00 p.m.

Juleika and I have a long conversation about her deep Muslim faith. We start discussing morality, heaven and hell, and, in particular, whether she believes it is possible for a good person, like Lynn, to go to heaven even if she is not a Muslim.

After some hesitation Juleika shakes her head and says no. "I am sorry, Tony, but only devout Muslims will go to heaven. You and Lynn, no matter how well you led your lives, are going to burn in hell."

She is sad to have to say this, and takes the opportunity to try to convert me so I will have a chance for heaven, even though it's too late for Lynn. Reluctantly, I tell her that she is unlikely to succeed, but I will think about it.

Then we realize that it is well past the end of Juleika's shift, so we check Lynn's diaper one final time (it is clean and dry) and Juleika says goodbye to both of us. Her week has ended; she is not due back for four days. We both know that she is unlikely to see Lynn again.

Now I am alone with Lynn, who is breathing peacefully beside me. This is too quiet for me, so I call my sister. We talk on speaker; Lynn hears every word.

Somehow we start talking about our early childhood, when we played together on Saturday mornings while our parents were still in bed.

"Do you remember how we would sit on my baby blanket and pretend it was a magic carpet?" asks Francie.

"Yes! We would tell each other what we were seeing down below."

"And when we watched cartoons on TV, we would start out in my room and then push the TV to yours when the commercials came on in the middle."

"We each wanted to watch it in our own room!"

"You would pull the plug from the wall because it was faster than pressing the switch."

"And then you held the TV to keep it from falling over while I pushed the cart as fast as I could."

"It did fall over once, when we went too fast around the corner to your room."

"It made such a crash! I was sure they would wake up."

"But they didn't. And when we plugged in the TV, it worked fine."

"I don't think we missed even a second of the show."

We laugh together at the happy memory. Then, still on the phone, I go into the kitchen to put away my dinner things, and while I am there Lynn stops breathing.

I am convinced that Lynn heard every word of those two conversations, even as she was simultaneously somewhere else. And I will be forever grateful that the last words she heard were the memories my sister and I shared, after which she felt comfortable enough to take the final step.

Francie is still on the phone when I realize that Lynn has died. She says, "You can't be alone when they come for the body." She and Paul drive in from Long Island to spend the night with me, and I go into the office to let our friends know.

Wednesday, February 24, 2021
www.CaringBridge.org/LynnKotula

My sweet Lynn—my Cutie—died at 8:00 tonight.

We were alone in the apartment, in the two-hour gap between the daytime aide and the nighttime aide. I needed company so I called my sister, and for quite a while I sat next to Lynn on the bed eating my dinner and talking on speakerphone. Lynn seemed calmer while Francie and I reminisced about happy moments from our childhood. Still on the phone, I walked into the kitchen to put the dishes in the dishwasher, and then suddenly thought, "I want to check on Lynn" and went back to the bedroom. During those few minutes, she left us.

I'm only sorry that I didn't realize the final minutes had come, and I wasn't able to hold Lynn's hand or stroke her hair at the very end. I so wanted to be able to ease her final passage. But I'm told this is fairly common in hospice deaths: The dying person waits until their loved ones are elsewhere before finally letting go. Or perhaps that's an old wives' tale.

In a few minutes, the funeral home folks will take away Lynn's body. I still can't quite believe it. I would love to have a few more quiet days like today to sit beside her. But I am glad for Lynn that this last phase went so quickly. For the first time in months, she did not seem to be in pain even once today.

40 comments

I don't think the part about leaving when people step away is an old wives' tale. It happened with both my parents and has happened with so many others. People do what they need to do. —Ann

Lynn's final few words were so interesting and meaningful. I will forever think of the dying process as a project requiring the utmost attention. —Linda

Lynn was not afraid of death. In fact, the week before she passed, she was kidding with me whether she is going to hell or heaven. I said, of course, heaven. Then she asked me what did I think heaven was like? And I said, "Well, I don't think you will find Jesus, but you'll be painting outdoors in a beautiful place with no bugs, no wind, just long shadows and a great cup of coffee that stays hot all day." — Maria Pia

After I upload the post, I am alone with Lynn for the last time. I stretch out beside her, stroking her hair, feeling her presence. The top of her head stays warm while the rest of her body cools. I talk to her as if she were still alive. "My dear girl," I whisper, smoothing her hair, "my dear, dear girl. I'm going to miss you so much. I can't believe you're gone." As if by speaking our love, I can extend it for a few more minutes.

By the time Francie and Paul arrive, Lynn's body is cool and gray, her face shrunken. I think this makes it easier for me when the undertakers put her on the stretcher. I cry as they take her, but at the same time I feel we have said our goodbyes—so many goodbyes—and this is just a body being removed at the end of the process.

As they are about to zip Lynn's body into the bag, one of them calls me over and points to her left hand. Tenderly I remove her watch and wedding ring. I strap the watch, a unisex Timex, onto my own wrist, the first time in years that I've worn one, and Francie puts the ring with the rest of Lynn's jewelry.

Francie and Paul, who have been through grief and loss far greater than this, tell me two wise things. First, you can't control grief. It comes over you in waves at unpredictable times, not necessarily when you are ready for it. And second, there is no rush. I don't have to do anything, discard anything, change anything in the apartment before I am ready. They also second my friend Ann's comment about needing to sit with my grief for a good long time. There is no way around that.

I listen and nod but find myself hoping that the events of the past months, the way Lynn and I worked together to draw her life to a close, will make this easier for me.

Friday, February 26, 2021
www.CaringBridge.org/LynnKotula

We went to bed around 1:00 a.m. and I crashed quickly, but at 5:00 a.m., I was up before the light, feeling Lynn's loss. I leaned over and smelled her pillow, breathing in her scent. As I lay back on my side of the bed, our big black cat, Boo, came over and put his nose against the same spot on Lynn's pillow. He sniffed repeatedly, then curled up against it and went to sleep; he remained there almost continuously for the next thirty-six hours. Lynn's cat, Lily, who surely misses her more than Boo, planted herself in Lynn's wheelchair. Both of them were bathing in Lynn's scent, as if they knew they would not see her again.

There is a window across from our bed that looks out toward the Hudson River; on the summer solstice the sun sets there. As Boo lay beside me and I was flooded with memories of Lynn, I realized that a large full moon was setting directly opposite our bed, framed by that window. The sky was clear, no haze or clouds, and the moon glowed a soft amber. I watched for ten minutes as it slowly sank into the horizon.

We have lived in this apartment for twenty-eight years and I've never seen this before. The moon never sets there; or if it does, I've never been awake to see it. I am an atheist and don't believe in reincarnation, but I was happy to hold contradictory thoughts and think that this was either a sign from Lynn that she was moving into a beautiful place, or perhaps Lynn herself, visible to me one last time.

After breakfast, the hospice nurse stopped by to see if I needed anything, and I told him about the tears on Lynn's cheeks. He said there's no reason to think they were anything other than normal tears, though he speculated (perhaps to comfort me) that they might have been tears of joy rather than sadness.

I will never know what Lynn wanted to tell me, but in hindsight, I think she was saying goodbye. I think she was saying how much she will miss me and the cats, her painting, and her friends. And I think those tears, which came a few minutes later, were real tears to accompany that very real sadness. But this is not a bad thing. It is the end of a life well lived.

Before they left, Francie and Paul accompanied me to Lynn's studio. I wanted to see how hard that would be while I had them at my side for support. We climbed the stairs, and I entered it for the first time in months.

In November, when I knew Lynn might be dying but still hoped the treatments would work, visiting her studio nearly broke me. Even more than our apartment, it is the place where you can most strongly feel her presence: There is an unfinished painting on the easel, decaying vegetables on the tabletop, and signs everywhere of an interrupted life.

I was calmer this time. We walked around the rooms for a while, looking at her still life setups and pulling paintings randomly from the racks. It felt okay. I can do this.

Then I put on my biking clothes and rode twice around Central Park for the first time in months. The sun was shining, the air mild, and it felt good. A first step towards resuming my normal life—or more accurately, finding my way into my new one.

22 Comments

I saw that moon the other night, too; it was amber with a lavender tinge, and I thought, It's telling Lynn, "Paint me!" —Laura

I do know that vision of clarity and beauty of the world, as if seen for the first time, when someone you love has passed away and you feel their presence everywhere. —Maja

Grief will come when it does, and you will deal with it. It is like a friend you don't want to see but need to see. In those times when it is hardest, you have friends to reach out to, and you will know them. —Tom

I am happy you took that bike ride and communed with the moon. Keep writing, if not for this CaringBridge, which has been a great gift for your friends, for yourself. —Monica

The moon outside my window

PART THREE

I Carry
Your Heart

First comes denial.

I tell myself that because Lynn and I got to say all those goodbyes, because she knew how much I loved her, because we had no regrets about our choices, my grief should be shallower or shorter than most. In post after post, I emphasize the positives—as when, just two days after she died, I describe riding around Central Park looking forward to my life ahead.

But, really, I am in shock, as when your body and mind conspire to shield you from the pain of an accident. For more than six years, I've been driven by one goal: To help Lynn stay as fully alive as possible. Now, in an instant, both the love of my life and the purpose of my life are gone. Suddenly I'm alone, and I don't know what to do.

When the shock wears off, I discover that in fact I am no different from anyone else. I am adrift in a merciless sea, and the grief will have its turn.

SHATTERED

Sunday, February 28, 2021
www.CaringBridge.org/LynnKotula

My desire for Lynn grows in the darkness. Each morning I wake before 5 and lie in bed thinking of her, talking to her, calling her back to me. I want the tears, I want the grief; they remind me of my love for Lynn and all the ways she changed me.

We have acres of medical supplies scattered around the house, stacks of unopened packs of adult diapers. There is a hospice sticker on the refrigerator reminding me not to call 911 under any circumstance. Taking it down, removing any of these things, would acknowledge that Lynn no longer needs them. I am not ready for that.

In a comment to a post I wrote shortly before Lynn died, our friend Ann offered a metaphor and prediction that I now hold close to my heart: that, after sitting in my grief for a long while, I will assemble the shattered pieces of my life into a new mosaic, one that includes Lynn (how could it not?) and allows me to move forward. It is no surprise that I am nowhere near that. I find myself moving between moments of calm and moments of extreme grief as if navigating between the shards, standing first on one and then another, trying to find my balance. But I am complicit in this. When I have felt okay for too long, I feel guilty. I am not ready to be at peace. I want Lynn with me, so I find another shard to stand on where I can feel her loss more keenly.

I kiss the hard plastic brace, now dirty, which supported her broken neck and cradled her head. I smell her pillow, where the scent is already beginning to fade. I take out my phone and scroll through the photos in which Google has kindly identified her face.

When I knew Lynn was dying, I started paying attention to the traces of her—her shirt draped over a chair, her toothbrush in its holder, her boots where we dropped them the last time we came home. I was trying to desensitize myself, knowing that once she was gone, these things would trigger my grief. So far that is working; I can look at them without crying. But grief finds its way in. Last night, friends in the building invited me for dinner. When I got there, I realized this was the first time I'd sat in their dining room without Lynn, the first time her place at their table was empty, and the grief welled up. I cannot desensitize myself from everything. I don't really want to.

Dr. Hellmann calls, introducing himself as "Matt." He tells me it was a privilege to work with Lynn and that he learned a lot from the experience. She taught him the importance of being "real" with his patients, that making mistakes is okay, so long as you admit them and do your best to correct them.

When we first met Dr. Hellmann, he was thirty-two and in his first year of full-fledged practice. We liked him, but Lynn was suspicious of his quiet and comforting manner, thought it was a trick he had taught himself in medical school. Over the years, through multiple crises, we came to treasure him, and though his manner never changed, I think it did become more heartfelt, more real.

During those years that he was growing in age and experience, the deepening might have happened anyway. But now he takes the time to call and say that knowing Lynn has been important to him. It is one more sign of a life well lived.

Monday, March 1, 2021
www.CaringBridge.org/LynnKotula

I wake again in tears; they come from nowhere.

During the day I feel surprisingly good. Lots of calls with old friends, some of us reconnecting for the first time in years. For hours I feel fine, thinking, I can do this, or This is working, but then I realize that I haven't started to do anything at all. I can't; nothing is working.

It's not just that I'm not ready to deal with all the supplies, clothes, and random stuff, it's that I can't figure out how to do it. I can't figure out how to do much of anything. I start the most trivial task—emptying the dishwasher, say, or cleaning the floor—and then realize, minutes or hours later, that I somehow abandoned that task having done almost nothing. I find the Swiffer leaning against a wall in some random spot and don't recall when I put it aside. I am living in the moment—and the moment keeps shifting.

I am thankful Lynn and I did not sleep touching each other. We would kiss goodnight (mandatory!) and then pull apart, careful not even to let our fingers touch because we each slept so lightly. (It was a huge change when we knew Lynn was dying and held hands in bed, wanting to touch each other every possible moment.) So now, when I wake in the night, I do not instantly miss Lynn's touch; I can drift back to sleep without the reminder of her absence.

I am also thankful that I have lived alone here for weeks at a time, when Lynn was an artist-in-residence in Italy and her various stretches of hospitalization and rehab, so the experience of being alone is not in itself devastating. It is only devastating when I remember that she is not coming back.

I had absolutely no idea when I went to bed last night that I would write another post, certainly not so soon. I didn't think I had anything to say. But I find myself doing it again. It is automatic, unplanned, as uncontrolled and uncontrollable as when I left the Swiffer standing against the wall.

14 comments

I'm afraid the grief is in charge. —Elizabeth

When it comes to mortality and loss, we're all in it together. We're just on different, unknowable schedules. —Naomi

I go on Facebook to see the responses to the notice I posted and am struck by how many of the comments are from colleagues at the law firm where Lynn worked as a part-time proofreader.

When Lynn was hired, she was in her early forties and already one of the older people on staff. In later years, she told me her younger colleagues barely paid attention to her, thought of her as "that old lady." She left the job seven years ago, but now dozens of them have taken the time to write about her. One says that even though his shift overlapped with Lynn's only one hour a day, he used to love their conversations during that hour. Another goes to Lynn's website and fills in the Contact Us form: "Lynn, you were beautiful, and I'll always treasure the few years that our paths crossed in this life."

During hospice I didn't have to cook and barely needed to shop. Friends stopped by frequently with care packages: neatly wrapped takeout meals and once an entire home-cooked dinner of roast chicken, potatoes, and vegetables.

When the food runs out, I go shopping for the first time. Only when I get home do I realize that I've bought enough for two. It's a complete surprise, and I start crying when I realize that half of it is Lynn's. But I go ahead and cook the quantities I'm accustomed to. I'm mimicking my habits of two but living in a world of one.

Tuesday, March 2, 2021
www.CaringBridge.org/LynnKotula

The days of crying for hours, unable to do anything else, seem to be passing. Now, it is more of a steady ache. But I am in a fog. This morning I couldn't figure out what day it is, and I still haven't finished the swiffering, despite passing that thing a dozen times a day, thinking each time I must sweep the floors soon; they are dirty and the cats keep shedding.

In 2012 my organization opened a facility in Brooklyn, and Lynn came to a big party there. We were walking through a hallway when a colleague snapped our picture; I put my arm around Lynn, and we smiled for the camera. The next week the colleague gave me a print, which I pinned to a bulletin board behind my desk, until another colleague saw it and said, "That should be in a frame." One day she snuck into my office and put it in a fancy frame she'd bought. It sat on my desk in Brooklyn for the next seven years.

I stopped working in that facility last summer and brought my things home in a shopping bag. Yesterday, I remembered the photo and went to look for it; I wanted to touch it and kiss her image. But I couldn't find it. I searched all over the apartment, eventually concluding that I must have lost it.

An hour later my phone rang. It was a colleague who shared my Brooklyn office, calling for the first time in months with a trivial work-related question. We started chatting and I told her about Lynn. She was sorry to hear the news, but then her voice brightened, and she said, "You know, I think of the two of you every day when I look at that lovely photo on the desk." Apparently, I had left it in a drawer, from which she resurrected it and put it where she could see it.

I started crying. I told her how much I missed that photo. She promised to send it, and a few minutes later my phone pinged. It was a text to which she had attached a snapshot of the photo, still in its frame. I cried again, heaving, and kissed the image on the screen.

I still can't believe she called me at that moment and happened to mention the photo. I think Lynn must have had something to do with this. Maybe I will start believing in the afterlife after all.

The photo my colleague texted me

During the day, I take care of business: bank, lawyer, finances. My head clears when I'm out of the apartment, when I have a purpose.

At night I am alone with my memories.

My sister says it is important to recall not Lynn the invalid but rather Lynn, my best friend and sweetheart, with whom I shared so many wonderful experiences. I know this is good advice, but I'm not ready to do that. My thoughts keep spiraling back to the last weeks of her life, recalibrating every detail of those intensive days. The process is painful, speculative, and keeps me tied to the past, but I feel compelled to work through it.

I write a post about 2020, the year Lynn's cancer began to beat the drugs, and then I write another that zooms in on the weeks before hospice: the eye exam, the final visit to Sloan when she was in so much pain. Then, the hardest of all, a long post in which I review Lynn's last two weeks in excruciating detail, capturing as many of the intimate moments as I can, wondering obsessively about what she was thinking and feeling as the days passed and her body failed.

It takes me three nights to write the post, repeatedly reliving those days as I remember more details and fine-tune the words. After I publish it, I walk around the house shivering uncontrollably, saying, "I did it, Sweetie, I finished it," as if Lynn had been looking over my shoulder the whole time. It feels like the most important thing I've ever written; it was certainly the hardest.

Then the second-guessing starts, which I write about, too. What if Lynn hadn't gone into the second clinical trial and instead we'd paid for the combination of drugs that Dr Hellmann offered? Would she still be alive today? What was Lynn thinking as her body failed? What were those tears really about?

Our friends assure me that with each step, we made the best choice we could, but it takes me weeks to reach a kind of peace.

Lynn's ashes in the urn

Sunday, March 7, 2021
www.CaringBridge.org/LynnKotula

I brought Lynn's ashes home yesterday. They are on the dresser, across from our bed, in what the funeral home calls a Classic Pewter Urn, surrounded by some favorite family photos. I could see it last night as I lay in bed reading, and again when I opened my eyes at first light.

I knew this day was coming, anticipated that it would be especially difficult, so I asked my friend Mark to meet me at the funeral home and bring Lynn back with me. He helped me choose the urn and where to place it in the apartment. I also asked some friends to invite me for dinner afterwards, because I was worried about being alone with Lynn's ashes for the first time.

But it turned out that I felt surprisingly calm, even flippant, when I left the urn with our doorman for a few minutes, saying, "I hope I'm not freaking you out, but that's Lynn in the shopping bag, so please take good care of her."

Mark and I had lunch together in the apartment, then walked on Riverside Drive to take in the chilly air. A jazz ensemble plays outdoors every weekend afternoon; for a while, we joined the crowd, and I danced in place to the music. Later, we saw two red-tailed hawks that live in our neighborhood. I always look for them but only occasionally see them, and only once before have I seen both together. I felt as if Lynn were close to me, making these good things happen.

When I came home after dinner, I realized that having the urn here made me feel calmer, not sadder. I talked to it as if it were Lynn herself, told her what a nice evening I'd had. This was not the first time I've spoken to Lynn since her death; I do it all the time, but before yesterday, I was either talking to her pillow in the morning or into the empty air, or, occasionally, talking to the moon as I did that first morning.

The moon has been waning for the past ten days, and as it gets smaller, talking to it feels increasingly sad. It reminds me that Lynn and my memories of her are moving away from me—and that this is a one-way trip.

In the morning, I was pleased to realize that I hardly felt sad at all. I spoke to Lynn in the urn, then leaned over and kissed her pillow as usual, but it wasn't a wrenching, cathartic experience. I cried for a few seconds and the tears melted away.

4 comments

I'm glad Lynn is home with you. I recently phoned and asked her how she was doing, and she said, "Don't even ask," and started to cry. There's no more pain for Lynn now that her ashes are in the urn. —Elizabeth

Elizabeth, I was with Lynn when you called . . . I could see that she lit up talking to you and how it seemed to calm her. —Maja

It turns out having your wife's ashes in an urn in your bedroom is no panacea. That's not to say it isn't helpful; it's just that when the tears come, there is no stopping them.

Monday, March 8, 2021
www.CaringBridge.org/LynnKotula

I have been crying floods since Lynn's retrospective show went online. The first time I tried to see the show, it took me an hour to get through the twenty-seven images.

My entire life with Lynn was bound up in and demarcated by her gallery shows. It seemed she was always either coming down from the high of one show or starting the long process of preparing for the next one. Would she have enough good paintings in time? Which ones should she hang?

She enlisted other artists to help with the choice, starting months or even years before the show. Sometimes she doubled down against opposition, as in: "I know most of my friends don't like this painting, but I do." And sometimes, her friends reinforced her feelings. If Lynn liked a painting and her friends did, too, that was perfect, it was in.

Then came the months of preparing, framing and hanging the paintings, and finally, the opening reception, where Lynn was the bride everyone wanted to congratulate. After all the angst about whether the paintings were as good as she hoped, there was nothing like seeing a dozen of them neatly framed on a well-lit wall and hearing friends and fellow painters congratulate her.

Lynn never believed the compliments, thought they were the sorts of things one typically said at an opening. She painted for herself—and continued to paint even when there were no shows on the horizon.

So here we are, with no more paintings coming, which breaks my heart. I know Lynn's physical life has ended, but how is it possible her artistic life has ended, too? I can't wrap my head around it. There will be a retrospective at Lynn's gallery next year, but that is a long time off, and I find myself crying at the thought that it will be her final show, even as I type these sentences. Thank goodness I am a touch typist and can keep going without seeing the keys.

13 comments

Years from now, Lynn's paintings will grace the walls of people not-yet-born, who will say to visitors, "I love this painting. It belonged to my great-grandparents, who knew the artist." —Mark

I begin to deal with Lynn's estate. It's pretty simple as legal matters go, but when I try to read the will, full of references to "my beloved husband," I have to stop and walk away to avoid getting it wet.

Condolence cards fill the mailbox, from close friends and, more often, acquaintances who don't read CaringBridge. Each one, no matter how straightforward or banal, sets me off. When I see the envelope, I think, Here we go again, and must plan when and where to open it.

Wednesday, March 10, 2021
www.CaringBridge.org/LynnKotula

This morning I interrogated my grief as I pulled myself from sleep. The grief felt a little far away, no tears pending. At first, I rather liked this, but then I wanted the tears, wanted the hurt. So I reminded myself of how Lynn used to say, "Hi Pussycat" at the start of every phone call, and that set me off. I was back with her, throbbing and sobbing and feeling close.

At the start of hospice, when I told the building staff that Lynn would not be coming downstairs again, I made a point of telling each person how much Lynn cared for him. The porter said that he already knew this because "she always talked to me," as if that were unusual. Another, Lynn's favorite doorman, the one she called her "big bear" because of the gentle way he helped her out of taxis, came up to see her in the apartment and started crying, then apologized for the tears. I had to assure him this was okay, that it was the greatest compliment he could pay, to cry in front of her.

It didn't surprise me that the doorman thought it wrong to cry, but I was surprised when two of the home health aides tried to cheer me up during hospice, saying they had seen patients rally from worse situations, or tried to move me to another room so Lynn wouldn't see my tears. I had to tell them that this was hospice, Lynn was dying, and we were here to help her have a good death, so of course tears would be part of the process. In subsequent days, both of those aides let themselves cry in Lynn's presence.

"Why do we grieve?" I ask on CaringBridge. "What purpose does it serve?" Unlike, say, the fight-or-flight instinct, it doesn't help me feed myself or make good decisions; on the contrary, it gets in the way.

I have already realized, many times, that I call on grief because it connects me to Lynn. Now, there is also a little voice saying that if I stop grieving too soon, it will prove that I don't love Lynn as much as I should. The grief is evidence that I am the man I want to be.

Another reason is that I am scared. Scared of losing Lynn as the memories become less distinct, and I confront the fact that I am living alone. But also scared in a more practical sense: Now that she is gone, what will I do with my life?

Here I am, sixty-five years old, and everything I know how to do, all the ways I know how to *be,* have been taken away from me. As the waves toss me about, I am able to live in the past with Lynn; my feelings for her are vivid and clear, and I don't have to think about moving forward.

Saturday, March 20, 2021
www.CaringBridge.org/LynnKotula

I've been using "waves" as a metaphor to describe the sudden arrival of fierce, piercing grief, a longing for Lynn so powerful that I have no option but to let the tears flow. (I've become adept at walking, cycling, cooking, brushing my teeth, even shaving with a blade while sobbing.) But just as in the ocean, beneath the waves is a tide, a tide of sorrow and longing that ebbs and flows with its own rhythm. When the tide is in, the waves are taller and stronger and crash with more force.

Yesterday, I tried to listen to the radio for the first time in months, and damn it, even the music betrayed me. Within seconds I felt a surge of intense grief and had to turn it off. The music connected me to a memory of Lynn in the Blairstown studio, standing at her easel while this same station played on the radio. We loved being in Blairstown together; Lynn would paint at one end of the hall, while I worked on projects at the other, the two of us sharing the music as it wafted through the house. It will be a while before I can play that station again.

Last night, I had dinner with friends, and although we toasted Lynn, we didn't otherwise speak about her. This seemed normal, even appreciated; I need to learn to go through life without constantly looking backwards. But when I got home, I began to cry again, wishing we had taken a few minutes to talk about what she meant to us, to call her into the room with words and memories. The grief reached a new level, and I started saying out loud, for the first time, that I wished we had died together, that it wasn't fair to be left alone.

Even while sobbing uncontrollably and saying, "Why did you leave me?" and "We should have died together," another part of me was looking as if from a distance, thinking these words sounded like a cliché. There is a scene near the end of *Schindler's List* in which Schindler, who single-handedly brought many of his factory workers to safety, starts pulling at the medals on his coat saying, "I could have saved another," if only he had cashed in these last few items. When I saw the movie, I hated this scene. It was so over the top. But now I realize that we can never predict the depths to which our emotions will pull us. It doesn't matter that I know my life isn't over; I would give up everything to be with Lynn again.

I was in the bathroom, looking at my scrunched red face in the mirror, trying to brush my teeth while saying, "I should have died with you," when Boo, our big black cat, jumped up on the sink, rubbed against me, and demanded that I pet him. This is why I need to stay, I thought. He doesn't fully understand what's happened, but he still has his needs, and I'm the only one here who can fill them. And petting him makes us both feel good.

12 comments

I remember when losing my mother to a brain tumor that the grief would flood me at all times. Anything triggered it, and it would only subside with time, as in a long span of time. In some ways, I think we only learn to handle grief differently in time, but it always stays with you. You will carry the memory like a rich, cherished presence. —Maja

Grief is an odd companion. After Richard's death, I once cried when I saw a cottage cheese commercial on TV. —Libby

Every time you write and express your pain, sorrow, and understanding, it helps me reach for my own feelings about this loss. Rip off those medals, we are all with you. —Laura

Mary Kay, the hospice agency's grief counselor, visits me, and we have a helpful conversation. It is good to hear my experiences reflected back by someone who has accompanied so many people through this process.

"It's common to spend several weeks in a state of shock," she says, "while simultaneously caught up in a thousand details: the funeral home, the memorial service, the bank, the friends who call. Then the noise dies away, and you start to realize that your loved one really isn't coming back—that this is it. This is your life now. This is what it will be. This is it."

Mary Kay terms what I'm going through "deep grieving," and confirms that I will have to sit with it for a long time. "Even though you and Lynn did everything 'right' and had no regrets about your choices, that doesn't make the grieving easier," she says. "Nothing makes it easier. The intensity of your grief is related to the intensity of your loss, whether that loss was a long, shared, intimate experience like yours or sudden, unexpected, and one-sided."

Mary Kay is tickled when I tell her how Lynn said, "I want you to have a girlfriend. No, I don't want you to have a girlfriend. Yes, I do want you to have a girlfriend."

"Girlfriend or not," says Mary Kay, "Lynn gave you permission to be happy again. This is a great gift. Not everyone is so lucky."

Saturday, March 27, 2021
www.CaringBridge.org/LynnKotula

The other day I received an email from an old friend who reads my posts:

> Harder for me to talk about is that I find myself
> wondering if I would grieve the way you are if
> Ann died. My suspicion is that I wouldn't have

the tears in the quantity you've described. I can picture myself stunned, looking around at what we shared, that toy dog, that coffee cup, that bed, and thinking, or feeling, what the fuck? Where did she go? Knowing my patterns, I assume I'd do what I've always done: sculpt, paint, draw, and perhaps I'd try to make those efforts in reference and memory of the one I love. But I can't anticipate my grief. Yours has been so continuous, so actual, and so graphically communicated that I'm almost intimidated, suspecting myself of not being a very emotional person. At this point, I can't imagine doing more than sitting in a corner and staring at the wall.

I replied to our friend that the crying has been a big surprise to me, too. It is only in these past few weeks that I've discovered how much crying I can do.

When the crying threatened to derail me yesterday, I decided it was time to start selecting photos for Lynn's memorial, confronting my loss in the most direct way possible. There are so many of them! When I first saw a good photo of Lynn, seeing it would make me terribly sad because we will never again share that experience. But if I looked away for a moment, maybe at another photo, and then came back to the one that made me cry, I could get past the tears and remember how we felt that day—and I might even smile.

Experiencing this with one photo did not make the next one any easier. The grief was just as overwhelming, and I had to go through the same steps again and again. Even so, I found the process surprisingly healing. I stayed up selecting photos for hours after my normal bedtime.

One of the cats has been peeing in the tangle of wires on the floor behind our TV, and the urine has soaked into the wood.

When I first started smelling the pee, I hunted all around the room without success. I thought I just needed to do a better job of cleaning the litter box. Then I smelled pee on the rug in front of the TV, so I scrubbed it thoroughly but still no luck. Finally, I dragged the carpet out of the room, pulled the TV stand away from the wall, and found the true source. I scrubbed the floor hard with only modest success, ordered something online that promised to do a better job, went to bed with the smell still hanging in the air, and woke up annoyed by it all over again.

An hour or two later, I realized that I'd barely thought of Lynn all morning.

I am convinced that the cat responsible for this is Lily, Lynn's cat, who is probably going through her own "this is it" process. Who is she supposed to nurse on now that Mommy is gone? How is she supposed to get the love she needs?

Thursday, April 1, 2021
www.CaringBridge.org/LynnKotula

I've been thinking about how grief serves as a connector: Two grieving people, each aware of the other's loss, will be more vulnerable and open with each other than normal.

I was talking to an administrative assistant at the firm that manages our retirement savings when suddenly she started telling me about how her father died a few years ago. Her mother had to sell the house and move in with one of her daughters because she could no longer stand to live in her own home. I had never spoken with this woman before, but we spent thirty minutes sharing stories related to our grief.

I exchanged emails with an acquaintance to whom I had sent an invitation to Lynn's memorial. I haven't seen her since we were children, but we reconnected by email when Lynn and I attended her stepmother's Zoom memorial last fall. I told her how much I appreciated the memorial, and she sent me a lovely note with a poem that had been part of the service. In response, I told her about e e cummings' poem "I carry your heart" that Lynn and I had chosen for her memorial. She replied "Oh Dear, Dear Tony, that poem means a lot to me. My husband and I selected it for our wedding thirty-three years ago. But last month, he told me that he wanted a divorce, so now we're figuring out how to live apart." Her words were openly emotional, and I realized that she is experiencing her own deep grief, losing her life partner just as I have lost Lynn. We connected because of our shared loss.

Then, this morning, I got into a long conversation with one of my mother's aides who lost her fiancé last fall. He died suddenly, unexpectedly, and within a few days two other friends of hers also died. Her grief was intense, and only recently has she been able to feel happiness. "For months, when I smiled, I was just going through the motions," she said. "And if I did have a happy moment,

SHATTERED 251

> I immediately felt guilty for doing so, and pulled myself
> back into the gloom where I belonged."
>
> I am lucky that Lynn gave me permission to be happy. I
> have a hard time getting there, and the feeling is often
> fleeting, but at least I know it is where I want to be.

For several weeks I have many conversations like these;
my willingness to connect with strangers surprises and
comforts me. One of these connections will change my
life.

∽

A friend sends me a short piece on grief that she says is
"all over the internet":

> It tears a hole through me whenever somebody I love
> dies... But I don't want it to be something that just
> passes. My scars are a testament to the love and the rela-
> tionship I had with that person. And if the scar is deep, so
> was the love. Scars are a testament that I can love deeply
> and live deeply and be cut, or even gouged, and that I can
> heal and continue to live and continue to love. And the
> scar tissue is stronger than the original flesh ever was.

Reading this, it occurs to me that it describes a form of
alchemy in which, over time, we transmute our grief into
something stronger and more valued—a kind of gold.

For a few hours, this thought makes me happy, and
I think, I can do this, but then my eye falls on a photo
of Lynn taken twelve days before she died. She is sitting
in her wheelchair looking up at the camera, a half-smile
on her face, with Lily the cat on her lap. Lynn is wearing

her neck brace and looks years older than she did a few months earlier, and you can see clearly how thin she is, how little is left of her body.

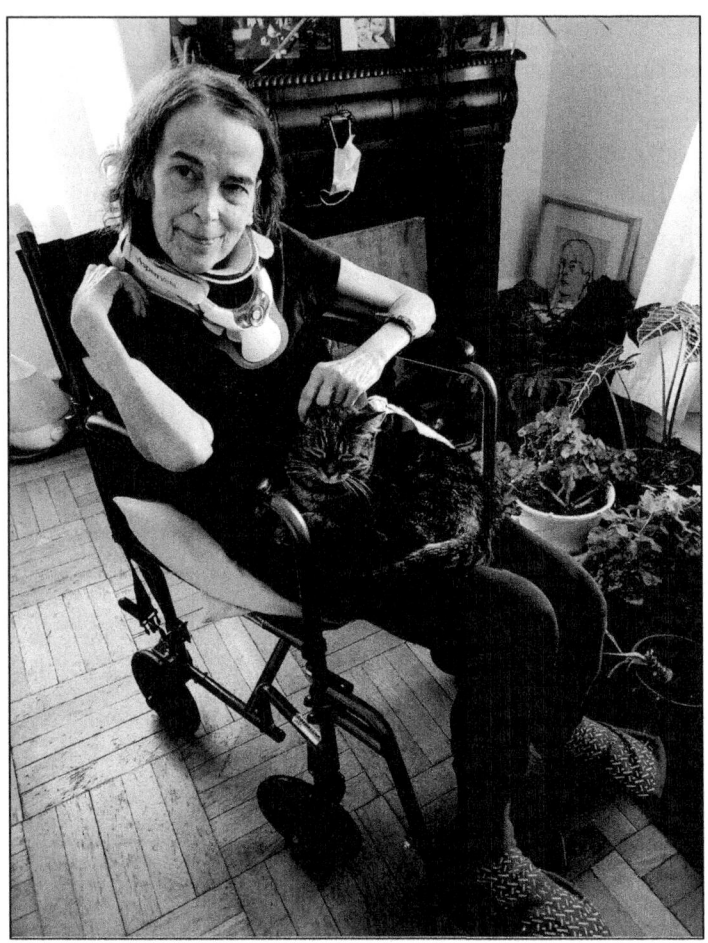

Lynn in her wheelchair, February 2021

I am drawn to the photo as if by a magnet. I can't stop thinking about how hard it must have been for her to maintain that smile when she knew her world was coming to an end. I quickly switch to another tab and stop looking at the photo, but by then everything in the apartment sets me off, and I cry continuously for an hour.

The next day I keep thinking about that photo, and every few hours I feel compelled to look at it again. Each time, my feelings shift—from their initial focus on loss and grief, to how hard it must have been for her to give me that smile, and then, eventually, to how strong she had to be to pull that off. Her body was ravaged, she knew she was dying, yet she pulled herself together, focusing her love and attention on whoever was there to receive it: me, visitors, phone callers, the cats.

Then, I remember that on the day I took the photo, our friends Sue and Arthur came to visit, and Lynn sat in the wheelchair chatting with them. Lynn was already losing strength and spoke slowly and in short sentences, but suddenly she interrupted herself to say, "Look behind me, Arthur, look on the wall," and she pointed to her left. She wanted to give Arthur the gift of letting him know how much she liked one of his paintings, that she had hung it where she would see it every day.

The first time I remember this, I cry. By the third or fourth time, I recall Lynn's strength, and the same memory starts to make me smile. The woman I loved was strong from the moment I met her. Right up to the end, she gave that strength to me and all her friends.

And that's when I realize this is the process I read about the day before: I am turning my grief into gold.

MAGICAL THINKING

A friend refers me to an online talk called "Grief After the Death of Your Partner" by David Kessler, whose website is Grief.com.

I normally avoid self-help experts, but, to my surprise, I like Kessler. He seems to know what he's talking about and has a nice soft touch. I am pleased to discover that many of the difficult issues that worsen grief don't apply to me, or at least, not much: Secrets that come out after your spouse's death; survivor's guilt; regrets in the form of second-guessing what you could or should've done differently; resentments; and well-meaning but obtuse comments by those who expect you to leave grief behind and get on with life. This is all good. It gives me hope that I will move through the deep grief as quickly as anyone could, which Kessler says will take at least two years.

Kessler also helps me feel better about something I have withheld from my readers, afraid of losing their support: I've been having long conversations with Cordelia, the woman I barely knew whose husband recently left her. Well, I can't say I barely know her now! We connected through our grief and have talked for hours, sometimes several times a day, and after each call I find myself eagerly looking forward to the next.

When I finally describe these conversations on CaringBridge, I emphasize the healing aspects. I don't mention our growing attraction, which I'm reluctant to admit even to myself.

Tuesday, April 6, 2021
www.CaringBridge.org/LynnKotula

Besides the loss of her marriage, Cordelia recently went through hospice with her beloved stepmother, spending twenty-three hours a day with her just as I spent twenty-three hours a day with Lynn. We have a lot to talk about: what hospice was like; what our spouses were like; what it feels like to be alone (except for pets) in a newly empty home; what we did this morning and what we hope to do next—all those tender details one shares with a close friend. I think Lynn had many such friends, but this feels new to me.

Cordelia and I are experiencing the joy of making a new friend at a time when we least expected it. When my first marriage ended, I started going out with other women as quickly as I could, looking for a relationship to prove that I was still desirable. Now, I'm more self-aware and neither of us is interested in dating. We are doing something more valuable, grown-up, and potentially long-lasting, which is to say, building a friendship.

It's been years since I had the time to make a new friend; Cordelia says it is the same for her. But here we are, rediscovering the fun of learning about someone new coupled with our own personal grief-group. It doesn't replace the grief or make me miss Lynn any less, but it is a lovely new piece in my mosaic.

4 comments

Connection to others is a lifeline. We need it like we need food and water. —Karen

Cordelia and I call each other every day, sometimes every few hours. It is intense, invigorating, even a little scary.

After a few days, she stops in the middle of a sentence and says, "Tony, are you feeling what I'm feeling? Because I've got a crush on you." It's one of the bravest things anyone has ever said to me. And I have to admit that yes, I do, too—the feeling is mutual.

Cordelia lives in Minneapolis but has family in the east. She's planning to come through New York next month, so we start talking about meeting in person and finding out whether we like spending time together. This is confusing and disorienting—and it makes me feel terribly guilty. I still talk to Lynn morning and night, cry for her every day, but now I find myself attracted to someone else? How can I admit this to our friends who read CaringBridge and fill every corner of my life? Aren't we all supposed to be sad now? Isn't Lynn's memorial just two weeks away?

The next day I meet two friends for a long-planned date at the Metropolitan Museum of Art. Pat and Mike are a couple, both artists, whom Lynn and I have known forever. While we are waiting in line, I summon my courage and tell them what is happening. Their response is better than I could've imagined: "Tony, this is great! It's exactly what Lynn would've wanted. We're so happy for you."

Then Pat turns to Mike and says, "When I'm gone, you go, Mike! You get out there and find someone!"

Friday, April 9, 2021
www.CaringBridge.org/LynnKotula

Cordelia and I continue to have long phone conversations that remind me of my giddy enthusiasm as a teenager, when I hogged the family phone for hours at a time. Cordelia didn't know Lynn, so she asks about her, and as I tell stories about our life, our friends, our travels, she chimes in to highlight the ways in which Lynn was a special person and how our relationship was so good for both of us. We are celebrating Lynn together. We are well aware of the pitfall—both of us on the rebound from profound loss—but we are following the advice of my therapist: "Don't run from it; don't run towards it."

I still cry for Lynn every morning, often while doing housework when my mind is free to wander. But the tears now have a milder quality, more spring rain than hurricane, and I welcome them because they assure me that I haven't stopped grieving. I find myself saying to Lynn, "I hope you're not jealous, Cutie, but you made this happen." By which I mean that Lynn made me the person I am today, so much more emotionally open than when we met.

I think I am starting to integrate my grief with the belief that there is joy ahead. It is amazing good luck that this is happening so soon, years earlier than I ever dreamed.

2 comments

I think it's a testament to your relationship with Lynn that you could make a new relationship. Your friends will accept whatever you decide to do next. —Elizabeth

I go to the dentist for a routine cleaning, and both he and the hygienist want to talk about Lynn. Eilat, the hygienist, tells me that when she saw Lynn in October, Lynn gave the impression that she knew she was nearing the end.

"She used hedge words when talking about the future," says Eilat, "*If* I have another appointment rather than *when*. That was the first time she ever suggested that her time was running out."

This is heartbreaking to hear, and I spend the afternoon obsessively thinking about it. At home, Lynn and I occasionally did say "if" rather than "when," but I thought that was like carrying an umbrella to ward off the rain. I always hoped there would be more time. And, especially, when Lynn agreed to have another spinal operation in December, I thought she was right there with me in that hope.

Now, I wonder if that was an illusion. Maybe Lynn was protecting me when she agreed to the operation; maybe she didn't expect to live but hid that from me, while allowing herself to be more open with the hygienist, a "safe" person who would not talk to any of her other friends.

I love Lynn for protecting me, and feel terribly sad that she felt the need to do so. But wasn't I also protecting her during the same period? Of course, I was. There were many times I shared doubts and fears with Frank that I couldn't fully share with Lynn. It is what you do.

᷍

My relationship with Cordelia continues to deepen, despite or perhaps because of the fact that we are 1200 miles apart.

We speak to each other for hours most evenings, and then again first thing when we wake, sleepy eyed with bed hair. Now we do video calls rather than just voice, especially in the morning. We like to see each other's faces, raw and emotional, as we pull ourselves from sleep.

We talk about how we feel and what we'll do during the day. I often find myself crying for Lynn while talking with Cordelia, sharing memories of our joy together, experiences I will never have again. Cordelia is supportive, helps me through the process, and then I support her as she shares similar feelings about the end of her long marriage. We are carrying our tigers together. But we also talk about mundane things. After getting up, we switch to voice-only, chatting about nothing much as we putter around making breakfast and getting ready for the day. It is a simulation of the casual intimacy of living together.

The more we talk, the more we realize this is not just a platonic attraction; there's an erotic tension between us that can't be ignored. Within days we start wondering what it will be like to have sex together, each of us for the first time in a long while. We share our sexual fantasies and discover that we are compatible: What turns me on, turns her on, and vice versa.

We assume we'll become lovers, at least for a while. Yet we can't really imagine how that will work, and we have no idea whether the physical connection will last for a day, week, month, or longer.

I try to write about this on CaringBridge, but I can't bring myself to click the Publish button. I'm afraid my friends won't understand how my love for Lynn can coexist with my growing attraction to this woman who has parachuted into my life. I continue to choose my words carefully when I mention Cordelia in the posts.

Tuesday, April 27, 2021
www.CaringBridge.org/LynnKotula

The memorial on Sunday turned out wonderfully, and not only for me: I have been flooded with emails from friends who want to share how much it meant to them. This is what I dreamed of, converting Lynn's life and joy into something useful for others, but I didn't expect it to happen now.

As for me, I feel completely supported, buoyed by the loving words of everyone who spoke or wrote to me afterward. Like Lynn, I have a hard time truly believing how many people I've touched in my life, and how much they care for me. But as with Lynn during her hospice period, when I think she started to appreciate how much she meant to so many people, it is becoming hard for me to deny all this love and support.

It doesn't hurt that Corde and I are having amazing, lengthy, life-affirming phone conversations. We are good for each other, and I'm happy we connected at this juncture in our lives. My Indian friend Dipti tells me she is sure that Lynn connected me to Cordelia, pulling strings from wherever she is. And who am I to say otherwise?

6 Comments

Yesterday's service had such a meaningful effect on me that I woke up a few times last night, and each time I saw, heard, and felt Lynn's strength, energetic enthusiasm, and intense focus. What a powerful spirit. —Alice

A friend gives me Joan Didion's book *The Year of Magical Thinking*, about the year after her husband's sudden death. It's the first time I've managed to read more than five pages of anything since last summer. Reading about someone else's grief, especially when the author is so gifted, fits right into my grieving process.

Not far into the book, Didion gives an example of what she means by magical thinking: She is trying to dispose of her husband's clothes but finds she cannot get rid of his shoes because, she realizes, she still hopes he will come back, and if he does, he will need shoes.

Reading this, I have an epiphany: I may have felt that way before, but not now, because if I thought Lynn was coming back, I couldn't possibly consider a relationship with Cordelia.

How easily we delude ourselves with logical thinking! For a few hours, I live in this fantasy, but then I start to realize that I absolutely do believe, at some deep level, that Lynn will come back. When I kiss her pillow or thumb through her clothes, it is not because I think she has left me forever, but because I want to keep my love for her alive while I await her return. Like Didion, I am caught in the irrational belief that Lynn may still walk through the door.

Then I reach a passage in Didion's book that summarizes her experience in a more formal way:

Grief turns out to be a place none of us know until we reach it.... We might expect if the death is sudden to feel shock. We do not expect this shock to be obliterative, dislocating to both body and mind. We might expect that we will be prostrate, inconsolable, crazy with loss. We do not expect to be literally crazy, cool customers who believe that their husband is about to return and need his shoes. In the version of grief we imagine, the model will be "healing." ... The worst days will be the earliest days. We imagine that the moment to most severely test us will be the funeral, after which this hypothetical healing will take place.... We have no way of knowing that the funeral itself will be anodyne, a kind of narcotic regression in which we are wrapped in the care of others and the gravity and meaning of the occasion. Nor can we know ahead of the fact... the unending absence that follows, the void, the very opposite of meaning...

When I first read this, I have to stop halfway through. Those early sentences resonate, reflecting my own experience during the weeks after Lynn died. My grief was overwhelming, but it wasn't linear and didn't feel rational; I started to feel better in the second week, much worse in the fourth. I was definitely a "cool customer" when dealing with various professionals, holding myself together in public before falling apart in private. And then there were those early days when I couldn't finish even the simplest task, and the powerful magical thinking that still prevents me from putting away most of Lynn's things.

But many of those events and feelings are behind me now, and when I pull myself together and finish the passage, I find myself rebelling against it. Didion's grief isn't the same as mine. I didn't "steel" myself for the memorial; on the contrary, I looked forward to sharing my emotions with friends and family. And I'm no longer feeling an "unending absence." Yes, I have moments of deep tormenting grief, sobbing in front of the mirror, but they come less frequently now and are interwoven with my growing sense that Lynn is here with me, in my apartment, in her clothes, in my heart. This is not absence; it is a deeply felt presence.

GRIEF AND JOY

When I finally meet Cordelia in person, she gets out of her car after driving eighteen hours in a twenty-three-hour period (totally crazy), and we hug each other with a ferocity that I've never before experienced. That intensity persists for several days, and when we try to figure out where it comes from, we realize that we are each parched for a kind of sustenance (love, comfort, joy; tenderness, friskiness, and gentle touch) that we can give each other. This is the rebound period, the rain after a long drought. It reminds me of my first weeks with Lynn, thirty-five years ago, and we are determined not to push it away but rather let it run its course.

Lynn and I had a satisfying sex life, playful and intimate, but it was rarely like this, and then her cancer made intercourse difficult and later impossible. In her final months, she became uninterested in sex, another way her body betrayed her. She felt bad about this and encouraged me to masturbate beside her, her hand on my thigh, sharing my pleasure even though she could no longer experience it. I was embarrassed at first, but I learned to enjoy it as if we were making love; it was the intimacy that mattered.

Cordelia and Tony in Central Park, May 2021

Cordelia has had her own dry spell, and during these days together we make up for lost time. This is exciting, fulfilling, and I am thrilled, again and again, to realize that what pleases me also pleases her. Then I look up from the bed and see Lynn's urn across the room and cringe, afraid of what she must be thinking. In my head, I assure Lynn that it's okay: I love her, nothing will change that, while outwardly I try to hide these thoughts from Corde and find my way back into the moment.

Of course, I don't mention any of this on CaringBridge.

Thursday, May 20, 2021
www.CaringBridge.org/LynnKotula

I've just spent five days with my friend Cordelia, and it is clear that we've embarked on some kind of love affair.

This is crazy and we both know it. Not because of what is happening between us but rather the timing: Lynn died less than three months ago and I cry deeply for her every day, while Cordelia and her husband finalized the terms of their divorce last week. I am nowhere near ready to reduce the huge part of my heart that Lynn occupies, or to take steps that would break the magical thinking and acknowledge she is not coming back. Her clothes hang untouched in the closets; I cannot bring myself to wash the pillowcase on which she lay for the last days of her life.

But this new relationship brings happiness and companionship, a warm and supportive ear, and hugs when the tears come. Despite superficial differences, Cordelia is a lot like Lynn in deep and important ways, so we talk about our feelings and try to understand this unexpected happiness that has come while we are both in the early stages of loss.

I quit my job about a week before Lynn's memorial. It was time. I love living day to day, spending my time solidifying old friendships and forming new ones, and planning for the celebrations of Lynn's art that lie ahead. Cordelia wants to help. She has already started to arrange her schedule to be part of the team that brings Lynn's memorial exhibition to life. I feel lucky to have her at my side.

2 Comments

Losing a beloved wife, quitting your job, and finding a new love in three months. Wow. But you have what many do not have—caring friends, a loving family, and a good therapist. Keep on keeping on! —Terry

You deserve some happiness and not to feel guilty about it. Even though you're wondering about the timing, maybe it is one of those things we cannot control. —Maja

For several weeks I spend my therapy sessions talking about the sex that Corde and I are having, which fulfills some long-suppressed desires and therefore feels like the worst possible betrayal of Lynn.

When Lynn first stopped being able to enjoy physical pleasures, it occurred to me that if she died sooner rather than later, I would still be a relatively young man and might be able to find a woman who would enjoy making love with me. Even this thought felt like a betrayal. I tried to ignore it, but it lodged uncomfortably in my brain, refusing to go away.

I talked about this with Frank more than once, and he assured me my feelings were natural. This was hardly the worst confession he had heard. What mattered was that I still loved Lynn and was fully committed to her.

Then Corde entered my life, and I discovered that she liked exactly what I'd been missing.

The ease with which Corde and I have sex ratchets up my guilt. How can I live with myself? Again and again, in my head and in my therapy sessions, I tell Lynn that I still carry her in my heart and that this pleasure, no matter how wished-for, doesn't replace my deep love for her.

It doesn't occur to me to stop having sex with Corde. How could I? But each time we go to bed, I have to overcome the guilt.

✌

I attend an online conference on happiness by *The Atlantic* magazine, with holistic speakers and also scientific presentations based on brain scans. They all say basically the same things.

First, it is possible to be happy and unhappy at the same time. Happiness and unhappiness are not mirrors of each other; they live in different parts of your brain.

Second, happiness is not something you can gain by setting and achieving goals; it lies within yourself. As Deepak Chopra says: "There is no point in chasing happiness. Happiness is chasing you. You just have to stop running and let it catch you."

And third, the most reliable way to experience happiness is through relationships.

I find all of this tremendously reassuring, especially the possibility that grief and joy can coexist like happiness and unhappiness.

Monday, June 7, 2021
www.CaringBridge.org/LynnKotula

How lucky I am to take this time, this summer, and just be.

I've been spending a lot of time in Blairstown, alone with my memories of Lynn. Somewhat to my surprise, I enjoy being here on my own. It is peaceful, meditative. Despite all the reminders of Lynn's absence, I think it is helping me to heal.

Today I turned off Lynn's phone, a deeply symbolic act that took a lot of strength. I kissed the phone and cried while doing it; saying goodbye is hard.

Now, when I cry, I realize it's because Lynn has gone somewhere without me, and I can't follow. That's so simple and universal as to be almost trite, but I find myself thinking about it over and over. In our thirty-five years together, Lynn and I were never apart for more than a few weeks, and we always knew we would be back together soon. Now, she is somewhere I can't access or even imagine, and I can never be with her again. Just typing that last phrase leaves me in tears, such is its power over me. A bit of religious faith would come in handy right now.

4 Comments

Although not popular in our twenty-first century secular society, it is possible to ask for a bit of faith. Faith does help one through. —Terry

It sounds like you are finding your way. We are listening. —Tony

Corde and a friend go canoeing near the Canadian border and are off the grid for five days—no phone, no internet. I spend those days obsessively thinking about her, realizing that I've become addicted to hearing her voice many times a day as if I were sixteen again. And I am terribly afraid that when Corde resurfaces, she will tell me she's come to her senses and no longer wants to be with me, which also reminds me of being sixteen.

When she's finally back online, Corde calls me at the first opportunity and shares that she's been thinking about me as intensely as I've been thinking about her. She kept a journal during the trip and wrote that she's fallen in love with me. This pleases me—how could it not? But it also scares me.

"I'm not ready to fall in love with you," I say. "It's too soon. I want to be a good friend, enjoy your company, and maybe over time something more will come."

"I know that," she says. "I don't expect you to feel the same way. Your love for Lynn, the joy you felt with her, is part of what I find so attractive. But that doesn't change how I feel."

Corde thrives in nature and wants to share it with me. She brings her outdoor gear from Minnesota and we go camping near the Appalachian Trail, the first time I've slept in a tent since high school. On the trail I have to stop short to let a large rattlesnake pass, and in the morning a bear visits while I'm brushing my teeth— vivid reminders that Corde offers new experiences, a different slice of life than the New York-centric museums and theaters I've known. I may never share her deep passion for the natural world, but at least I can get a taste of it, see it through her eyes.

Corde also brings an appreciation for mindful meditation and the teachings of Thich Nhat Hanh, the Vietnamese Buddhist monk who popularized mindfulness before it was a buzzword. Each morning we ring a prayer bell and read from his Everyday Peace Cards that contain short lessons to help you live your life, with titles like "Water the Right Seeds" and "I Am Here for You."

Some of the principles are fundamental: live in the present moment; pay close attention to the world around you; befriend your difficult emotions; death is not an ending but a transition into another phase. These feel familiar, and one day I realize that Lynn followed them as an inherent part of her nature. She was always fully present with everyone she met, the hours she spent looking at her still-life setups were like mindful meditation, and she was not afraid of dying.

I've been absorbing these precepts ever since we met; now they are helping me get through the day.

∽

In July, friends organize a small retrospective of Lynn's paintings at a gallery in Cold Spring, New York. It is a group show, *Affinities: Lynn Kotula and Friends*, featuring works by Lynn and seven other artists whom she influenced over the years.

When I tell one of the artists that Cordelia will accompany me to the opening, she says, "Well that will be ... interesting," leaving me to wonder what she means, although I think I know. This will be the first time that Corde and I are together at an event devoted to Lynn, filled with her friends.

I mention our conversation to the artist's husband, and he is sympathetic. "She just needs more time," he says. "Not everyone is ready to accept Cordelia. It's too soon."

Lynn's sister comes to the opening but flinches when I try to kiss her and then studiously avoids Corde and me by staying on the other side of the room. I can see how painful it is for her to see us together.

I want to tell her that it's not so simple: I still love Lynn, and Corde is helping me navigate my grief. But this is neither the time nor the place, and I'm not sure anyone here would understand.

> *Wednesday, August 18, 2021*
> www.CaringBridge.org/LynnKotula
>
> Lynn died six months ago next week. I can't decide whether that feels like five minutes or an eternity.
>
> These past few weeks I've been more keenly aware of her loss than at any other time since the memorial. Four, five, six times a day something sets me off and I start crying uncontrollably. This happens at inconvenient, potentially dangerous times: while driving on winding roads, or riding my bike downhill. I learn to go with it. The tears will pass; I just have to blink faster and hang on.
>
> The crying happens despite the fact that I am building a solid relationship with Cordelia. We've now spent weeks at a time together: in Blairstown, in coastal Maine with her father, at her house in Minneapolis. We've moved past our early infatuation to the part where we bump up against each other, grow annoyed, and talk things out.

Sometimes our bumping is literal. Corde and I have each developed our own domestic choreography, but I haven't taught her mine and hers baffles me. As I pivot from sink to fridge or empty the dishwasher while she makes breakfast, I often find her standing exactly where I want to be. I am constantly bumping into her, annoyed to find her in my way.

Mostly I am annoyed because Corde is not Lynn. She is a warm, caring person who (like Lynn) talks to strangers and makes them feel comfortable, and she's done some amazing things: She's run for public office twice, was president of her neighborhood association, and spearheads volunteer projects all over her corner of Minneapolis. But she doesn't have Lynn's ease in the world; her smile doesn't come as readily, and she doesn't know the steps to my dance.

At home, Corde often looks quite serious, no trace of a smile. It's the same expression Lynn had when she was angry at me. Again and again, I feel threatened. Who is this woman living in my house? Will she always be like this? But I can't figure out how to lighten the mood. I find myself making stupid jokes, silly things that fall flat and have the opposite effect.

When I finally muster the courage to talk to her about this, Corde looks at me thoughtfully and says: "You know, Tony, I'm very earnest." If I want to have a relationship with her, I need to make peace with who she is.

Then she tells me about the things I say and do that push her away, many of which I feel that I, too, can do little about.

Still, I remain hopeful. Corde understands me deeply; she has a knack for saying exactly the right thing at the right time, and sex together is exciting and fulfilling. It's as if we are connected at two ends of a spectrum—emotional intimacy and physical intimacy. But we are having a hard time conquering the middle ground, the thousands of small interactions that make up a day.

One day, when I've been crying, Corde says something particularly helpful, and I blurt out, "We have to make this work! We could spend years looking for the perfect partner and never do better than we're doing now."

I tell Corde about two Indian friends, Mini and VJ, whose marriage was arranged by their families. "One year, Lynn and I celebrated New Year's Eve in India with a dozen of Mini's cousins—doctors and professionals—all of them in arranged marriages. They spent the whole evening trying to sell us on the idea! Apparently, it's not the initial attraction that matters, but rather the years you spend together, and having the support of your family and friends."

Corde doesn't seem terribly convinced.

"Maybe we can learn something from them," I continue, trying to persuade myself as much as Corde. "We just have to give it time. The rough edges will smooth. Eventually, we'll learn to dance."

〜

In late August, I am riding my bike on a country lane when a large dog races out, sinks his jaws into my leg, and shakes his head as if I were a rabbit. A vascular surgeon operates to convert the multilayered, multipuncture bite into a three-inch wide and three-quarter-inch deep crater that can be properly cleaned, but by then a major infection has set in. I spend five days in the hospital on IV antibiotics. In the long run, this is just an annoying flesh wound, though that does seem an understatement.

Cordelia changes her plans and comes to Blairstown to help me. I am so lucky! When we return to the city for the first time since May, she starts the hard work of cleaning up the apartment. I don't ask her to do this; she just does it, months sooner than I could've managed on my own.

There are messes everywhere, dozens of prescription medications that are no longer needed, small piles of Lynn's clothing in the corners. You can see the bones of the apartment and the beautiful views, but it doesn't feel as welcoming as Lynn would have wanted.

Cordelia brings everything to me so we can discuss what to keep and what to discard. I am emotionally incapable of doing this; in fact, I am often in another room while she spends hours pulling out things that had been stuffed into closets or spilled over onto available surfaces.

Cordelia pulling out bags that had been
crammed under the counter

We consolidated Lynn's clothes into a closet and a bureau, unearthed her beautiful scarves and handbags, and put them in a couple of baskets in the living room. We went through her family photos, collected her sketchbooks into one pile, and flipped through years of drawings.

The whole process was immensely sad. Every day brought dozens of touchstones of our shared life: photos that I examined, perfumes that I sniffed, and handwritten notes that I read until I couldn't bear to read further. I was sad from morning to night and cried frequently. But it also seemed necessary. The longer Cordelia worked at it, the better the place felt, until it reminded me of the apartment as it used to be. And in doing this, Cordelia and I were constantly talking about Lynn: what she wore, how she moved in the kitchen, how she interacted with all these objects. Again and again, Cordelia said she was getting to know Lynn through this process.

One morning we lay in bed talking. I said I had felt sad from the moment I awoke, and Corde said, "Yes, I feel that way too." I assumed she was thinking about her divorce, but she said no: "I realized that I've been cleaning and fixing up the apartment not only for me but also for Lynn, so that Lynn will smile when she walks in the door, will sit down, and feel comfortable. And it just hit me that she's never coming back." The magical thinking was affecting Cordelia, too.

That was a week ago. Corde drove back to Minneapolis, leaving me alone here for the first time in several months, and instead of feeling worse, I've felt stronger each day. I passed through a storm of grief and memory, but now, at least for a while, I can enjoy being in the home that Lynn and I created.

Years later, I will remember what I omitted from that post.

Before we accepted that she was dying, but after things started going very wrong, Lynn began tracking her vital signs. We bought a blood pressure cuff, a pulse oximeter and a fancy thermometer, and Lynn used them four times a day, carefully recording the results in a small notepad along with each bowel movement and pain pill.

Every time her blood pressure spiked, we'd think, Oh no, this is it, the drug has stopped working. Then her vitals would return to normal, and we'd breathe a sigh of relief.

When we saw Lynn's doctors we brought the notes with us, but really, we wrote them for ourselves. We wanted to believe that she was getting better, and we hoped these records would demonstrate that we were going in the right direction.

Corde brought me that notepad. I knew it was something special: page after page in Lynn's distinctive handwriting. But I couldn't bring myself to read it. Remembering our hope was just too painful. I put the notebook away somewhere, and when I wrote the post on CaringBridge I didn't even mention it.

Corde loans me her copy of *Being Mortal* by Atul Gawande, a wonderful book in which he discusses exactly the kinds of choices that Lynn and I made. Gawande confirms that we got it right in important ways: We found a caring oncologist, we signed up for palliative care early on, and when we opted for home hospice, she was able to die peacefully, surrounded by love.

But we came close, so close, to getting it wrong in the end. Gawande says it is common for the families of dying people to want more aggressive care, and often the patients allow themselves to be talked into going back to the hospital to please their loved ones. Lynn and I experienced this dynamic when the surgical team wanted her to come back for brain radiation and she said, "I'm not going back tomorrow; I need at least another day at home." Lynn was the patient, and I was the family member who pulled her towards more treatment. If Dr. Hellmann hadn't called when he did, I might have convinced her to go back.

My father died in a hospital, strapped in a bed and unable to talk with a breathing tube down his throat. I swore I wouldn't do the same to Lynn. But look how close I came. It is a sobering thought.

When Cordelia returns to New York, so does my grief.

Frank tells me this is a good thing. He says he worried during the spring and summer that if I didn't take the time to fully sit with my grief, this would haunt me later. No worries about that now!

From the minute I kiss Corde at the airport, I feel myself pulling back. Everything she does annoys me. This is partly because I've grown used to being alone in the apartment, regained my rhythms, and her arrival disrupts them. But there is something else: When I try to hug or kiss her, I feel like I'm betraying Lynn. I thought I'd gotten past that, but here it is again.

After a few days, Corde says I've been acting distant and asks, "Where did you go?"

"I don't know," I say. "But I agree, something is wrong."

We examine our feelings, laying them out on the table.

"I'm having a hard time maintaining my balance," I say, "trying to grow with you while hanging on to my love for Lynn. I'm not sure I can do it. At least not now, and maybe not for a long time . . . and not if I feel pressured to say that it's happening before I'm ready."

"I understand," says Corde, "but I need to be loved, too, and I'm not sure you will ever be able to love me the way you loved Lynn." Then she leans forward and takes my hand. "But there's something special between us, I feel it too, so I'm willing to be with you while you're in this place—at least for a while."

By the end of the conversation, I feel attracted to Corde again, excited by our intimacy, and that night we make love for the first time in several days.

I start giving away some of Lynn's possessions, first offering a few items to her sister, then some Indian scarves and clothing to friends who happen to be visiting. This gives them so much pleasure that I write a CaringBridge post inviting any friends who would like one of Lynn's scarves to contact me. It makes me happy to think of Lynn's friends enjoying her special scarves, remembering her when they wear them.

As for Lynn's paintings, their time will come—starting with the memorial exhibition planned for next summer.

The idea has been growing on me for months, expanding in scope each time I think about it. Lynn left a legacy of beautiful paintings. I don't want them to rot away in storage; I want to share them with the world. Better than any memorial, this will ensure that Lynn lives on in other people's hearts.

Corde accompanies me to Lynn's studio, and we brainstorm the tasks that lie ahead: inventorying and photographing the paintings; finding a writer and designer who will create a beautiful catalog; selecting the pieces that will be in the show; running a publicity campaign; and then, finally, framing the paintings and hanging the show. It's a big project.

Tentatively, Corde asks whether I can use her help even though she's never done most of these things before.

"Absolutely!" I say. "I don't see how I can do it without you."

Later Corde tells me that this was a watershed moment, the first time I've asked her to help me create something together. She decides to spend more of the winter in New York in order to be as available as possible.

Friday, December 3, 2021
www.CaringBridge.org/LynnKotula

Recently, I've been distressed to realize that my sense memory of Lynn is slipping away. When I try to remember how it felt to touch her waist, smell her hair, or nibble on her shoulder, I largely can't. Many of these memories are being replaced by my current knowledge of how Corde feels, smells, and tastes. This makes me terribly sad. I don't want to lose any part of Lynn; I want to hang on to her and build my relationship with Corde at the same time. But that's not possible. We don't get to keep all the sensory details of our deceased loved one; we have to let some of them go.

When I told Frank about my distress, he described the sense memories as "ephemera" and said not to worry: The deeper connection between Lynn and me is unchanged. But he was glad to hear that I've saved a few of Lynn's voicemails, mundane messages like, "Hi Pussycat, I'm at the market. Do you want me to get some eggplant?" When I want to wrap my arms around her and hold her close, I play those messages and look at the memorial slide show. I'm just sorry we didn't make any videos.

Tomorrow, December 4, would have been Lynn's seventy-sixth birthday. Even though I am doing well, I miss her every day.

⌒

During the holiday season, I start thinking about love and loss. Not only does the calendar call out to me (Lynn came home from the hospital ten months ago and died exactly two months later), but so do the rituals of the season, each of them reminding me of Lynn's absence. And now there is added pressure because my brother-in-law Paul, who has been living with stage IV cancer for almost three years, is confronting the fact that the drugs that kept him alive have stopped working. Absent a miracle, he will not see another Christmas.

On a gloomy Saturday afternoon, Francie, Paul, Corde, and I drive out to St. John's Memorial Cemetery in Cold

Spring Harbor, Long Island, where many members of our family are buried. It is an unusual place: moss-covered groves in an undulating landscape, with gravestones positioned almost randomly in small clusters. I haven't been here in years, but I want to visit my father, brother, and nephew Peter—and, most importantly, think about what it would be like to visit Lynn here.

The cemetery feels beautiful and healing. I think that I will eventually move Lynn's urn to this spiritual place, where now and then relatives and strangers will see her marker and think (or speculate) about her. But it takes me by surprise when I say this aloud and Paul responds: "Maybe next year, the three of you will visit me here."

All we can do is hug each other and cry.

Francie and Paul enter the cemetery

A week later I learn that my first wife has died of pancreatic cancer, which strikes me as a surprisingly bitter loss. The two women with whom I spent my adult life are both gone now. A large part of my past has suddenly been erased.

In late 2020, Deborah contacted me to tell me of her diagnosis. I replied that she and Lynn were on parallel tracks because Lynn's cancer was back, and now we, like Deborah, needed to find a new treatment.

Deborah started reading my CaringBridge posts and continued doing so through the months that followed. In her last email to me, when she was feeling happy because her scans looked good, she wrote:

Dear Tony, thanks for sharing your emotions. I admired the way you and Lynn handled the last months, days, and hours of her life. I'm trying to follow her example. Hugs, Deborah.

Shortly thereafter, her treatment stopped working.

I am moved by the idea that Lynn's example helped Deborah and is now helping Paul, who is living his last months much as Lynn did, taking advantage of every moment for as long as he can. I don't know if reading our posts played a role, but I am happy Paul has reached this equilibrium. And terribly sad, as I watch him energetically playing with his five grandchildren, knowing his time is running out.

∽

Monday, January 24, 2022
www.CaringBridge.org/LynnKotula

Today marks eleven months since Lynn died. I've come to appreciate this "year of mourning," time that I've given myself to experience grief without trying to control it— and without pushing myself to figure out what I'm going to do or who I'm going to be for the rest of my life.

Paul died sooner than we expected, at home with his family, reconciled to his passing and talking openly about his life and feelings, similar in outline to Lynn, but the specifics were different. Lynn faded for almost a week, saying she had "a lot to do" but unable to tell me what that meant. Paul, on the other hand, was explicit on the subject: His pain was increasing, he'd said his goodbyes, and there was no reason to stay in his body any longer.

In hindsight, I think Lynn was just as ready as Paul. When our bodies betray us and there is no hope, it is, surely, a relief to leave.

After Paul died, Corde and I printed out some recent photos of him that we gave to family members. This inspired me to print some of my best photos of Lynn. I now have pictures of her in every room, except the bathroom. (I'll have to work on that.) I love having Lynn with me everywhere. Rather than tie me to the past, I feel that it frees me. If I have Lynn with me externally, I don't have to hold on to her so hard internally. I can make more space in my heart.

Corde is staying here this winter, and I promised that I would free up some space so she would no longer be living out of suitcases. But when the time comes, I still can't do it, so she takes the lead and helps me. We go through all of Lynn's more mundane clothes—underwear, jeans, and cotton turtlenecks. Some of these fit Corde, and she says she would love to wear them if doing so won't freak me out. I like seeing Corde in Lynn's black jeans or orange turtleneck, and I think Lynn would have liked this, too. It is practical to use them, and Lynn was very practical.

The rest of Lynn's clothes are in bags waiting to go to charity, except for some signature items that she wore at art openings. These are hugely important to me; I love to run my hand over them and remember Lynn wearing them.

For months I've worried about how I am going to part with them, but suddenly I realize that I don't have to; I can keep them here for as long as I need them. So we take those hangers and move them into a closet that I use on a regular basis, and every time I open that closet, there she is.

♫

Wednesday, February 23, 2022
www.CaringBridge.org/LynnKotula

A year ago yesterday, Lynn said her last coherent sentence: "Don't bother me, I've got a lot to do." A year ago today, she refused food and drink. A year ago tomorrow, she took her last breath. When I first thought about this post, I expected the next sentence would be about the passage of time, but this morning I find myself plunged back into the immediacy of those days, as if I haven't moved past them.

The flashbacks began on February 3rd, when I realized that it was exactly one year since we spent a torturous day getting Lynn's vision checked. Then again on February 9th, exactly one year since Lynn and I decided to stop treatment and begin hospice. I couldn't stop thinking about all the pain she endured as we tried to find a way forward. It's not her peaceful departure that I find myself revisiting, but rather the difficult days on the way there— her strength, her bravery, her hand clutching mine.

But that's also the best part. In all the years we knew each other, we were never more in love, never more present for each other, than in those final weeks. Even when part of me tries to second-guess our decisions—Could we have avoided all that pain? Should we have started hospice earlier?—I know we got the most important things right.

Cordelia lives here much of the time now; we make love in the same bed where Lynn and I made love, surrounded by photos and paintings and memories of Lynn. It has taken me a long time to make peace with that. I am, after all, still deeply in love with Lynn. And I don't want Lynn to think I am cheating on her—physically or emotionally. I don't want her to think that I am having more fun with Corde than I did with her.

In the first few months with Cordelia, I was concerned about this. I frequently talked to Lynn directly to reassure her that I loved her more than anyone, that no one could ever replace her. But you can't keep doing that forever. Over time I became more comfortable with having two women in my life, and now I talk to Lynn as to an old friend who is watching and encouraging me.

Which still doesn't make it easy. I measure everything Corde does against my memories of what Lynn and I used to do, here in this same space. I need to stop doing that. I need to hold Lynn in my heart while being open to what the present brings.

4 comments

I was looking at the group photo of Bowery artists on the gallery's website this morning. I had a good long look at Lynn smiling with her familiar red hat atop her head. It warmed my heart to see her. I picture her in the same way, with that same warmth, love, and kindness in her smile, up wherever she may be, looking down at you and Cordelia. —Steffi

⌇

Corde and I spend the spring preparing for Lynn's retrospective exhibition: *Lynn Kotula: A Life in Painting 1984– 2020.* It's a wild ride. We are on a treasure hunt, looking not only for the paintings that will be featured in the catalog, but also for any scrap of writing that illuminates her creative process.

Lynn didn't like talking or writing about her work; she wanted each piece to speak for itself. But when she did, she was simple, direct, and eloquent. I know her words are here somewhere, I just need to find them.

Every morning I wake up energized and excited. I read everything in Lynn's notebooks and on her computer, searching for the diamonds. In my mind we are resurrecting Lynn, the essential Lynn, the artist who couldn't stop painting.

I return to the studio again and again with Cordelia and our artist friends, selecting and photographing the best paintings. I spend more time there than I ever did when Lynn was alive. It becomes like a second home to me, her art infusing my every pore.

Working on the catalog and updating Lynn's website, I feel more in touch with her than at any time since the memorial. I marvel that my feelings are as intense as a year ago. Frank thinks that I will be better off for having lived through this experience—even if, sometimes, I feel like I'm tied to the past.

The entry to Lynn's exhibition

Wednesday, August 31, 2022
www.CaringBridge.org/LynnKotula

When I wrote the last post, I was deep into preparations for Lynn's show, surrounded by her life's work. It was an exhausting, exhilarating time. Many friends came to the show, and most importantly, we visited with Lynn through her paintings.

A few weeks later, I noticed that I felt different, stronger. I thought perhaps the show had served as a watershed event, bringing closure. But I don't believe in closure, that's too much like magical thinking. I don't want to close out my grief any more than I want to close out my memories of Lynn.

I think simply by living, I laid down new memories which superseded the ones that used to trigger me. Eighteen months have passed, during which I've cleaned the house dozens of times without crying and gone swimming with Corde probably as often. Now I am cleaning the house for me or for Corde when she is here. Now when I go swimming, I have happy memories of swimming with Corde alongside my happy memories of swimming with Lynn. All these new memories sit on top of the old ones, like planks of new flooring. The more of them I lay down, the more solid the floor. The grief remains, but it is one floor further down, and every day I add more planks on top of it.

The other day I was driving alone to Catfish Pond, a beautiful lake near Blairstown where Lynn loved to swim. I looked over at the empty passenger seat and imagined Lynn sitting beside me. "Hi Cutie," I said. "We're going swimming. Corde is away, so you can keep me company." Tears filled my eyes as I drove up the final stretch to the parking area, but they felt good.

5 comments

Thank you for keeping us involved as you wend your way thru this grieving period. Your words have helped me so much as well. —Anne

You are so right about the healing capacity of time, but it is a long process. The richness of your memories will also surface at some point in time, as we seem to forget the painful ones. Maybe it's necessary in order to continue our lives. —Maja

Lynn taught me a great deal about living as fully as possible in the face of a deadly disease. Then she demonstrated transitioning to the hereafter with enormous strength and grace. When my turn comes, I hope I can follow her example. —Naomi

〜

We are going to bury Lynn's ashes on Thanksgiving weekend, at the cemetery in the woods where my father and grandparents are buried. On the same day, at the same time, we will bury my brother-in-law Paul's ashes. It will be a joint ceremony, a private family event.

Left to my own devices, I might have kept Lynn's ashes in the bedroom for years. I've come to enjoy seeing her there, the silver urn with her signature red hat and glasses on top and one of her favorite scarves wrapped around the base. I've said good morning to her many times.

But when my sister tells me that she wants to bury Paul while her daughter's family is in town, I decide to bury Lynn then, too. Even though I don't believe in closure, I think burying Lynn, saying a formal goodbye, will help me move into the next phase of my life.

What that next phase will be, I don't know. Corde and I continue to spend much of our time together and have a lot of fun and adventures, but these past eighteen months have been, in some ways, a detour from our normal lives. Neither of us is working in the traditional sense, and much of our time together is spent on projects that will not carry forward. We don't know what it will be like to live together when we're doing separate things. And there are still stretches when we realize that we're not pleasing each other, when the space between us goes unpleasantly silent, and we wonder whether this relationship can sustain us over the long haul.

Thursday, November 10, 2022
www.CaringBridge.org/LynnKotula

Francie, Corde, and I drove out to the cemetery to select the sites for Lynn and Paul. I was moved to see the markers for my father, brother, and Francie's son, Peter, and to think that soon Lynn and Paul will be beside them. Then I got down to business, pacing out the space.

A few days later, Corde said that I'd been distant again and wanted to know why.

"You're right," I said. "Since returning from the cemetery, I've been talking to Lynn in my head, repeatedly assuring her that she is and will always be my true love."

Corde touched my arm and said, "I understand, but I need someone who feels and speaks about me the way you just spoke about Lynn. Lynn can't be your one and only true love forever if you also want to have a relationship with me. You need to find room in your heart for both of us."

This has been a recurring theme since the start of our unexpected and improbable relationship. For eighteen months we've let these moments pass. I don't think we can keep doing that for much longer.

Corde drives off for a long-planned visit with a friend, and I spend a few days with just the cats for company. After the immediate sense of loss—what happened to that nice warm woman who was sharing my bed?—I settle into my rhythms again.

One morning as I walk through the living room, I glance at a photo of Lynn looking happy and cute in front of one of her paintings.

Lynn before the opening of her 2012 show

It's a photo I've seen hundreds of times, but today it sets me off. The tears flow until I cry myself out.

Then I realize what I need to do. I need to write a letter to Lynn. I need to tell her what I've been feeling and assure her that she will always have a place in my heart no matter what happens between Corde and me. Exactly the kind of romantic mush that we never wrote to each other and almost never said out loud, because Lynn hated that kind of thing. But now I need to say these words loudly and clearly. And then I will bury the letter with her, so she will have it forever.

I sit down at the computer and start typing.

Dearest Lynn,

I want you to know that just because I am burying you, does not mean I want you out of my life. On the contrary. I carry you in my heart, and I want to keep you there forever. I doubt that I will ever again be as relaxed, comfortable, and smitten with anyone as I was with you. I still feel that way about you—smitten—and so sad you are not here with me to share our life, to make me feel whole and create beautiful art and cook tasty new recipes. Because the world needs beauty, attention, and care, and that's what you gave us.

You breathed life into me.

Now, I hope to support Cordelia, breathe life into her, and enjoy good times, just as you and I had together. I don't know what will happen. But in order for us to have a chance of success, I need to make space in my heart. I want the next chapter of my life to be as rich as the years you and I shared. It may take a while, but I want to give it a chance.

So I will move your ashes out of the bedroom and put them in a beautiful place, but I will keep photos of you all around me, with your bright smile and impish excitement, and I have covered the walls with your paintings. I will hold you and honor you in every fiber of my being. I honor you each time Corde and I rub noses and exchange breath, each time we talk about difficult feelings, each time I fuss over a meal and try to make a balanced, attractive plate, each time I savor a bite of that meal. You are in me, my love, in specific and tangible ways. Nothing will ever change that.

So goodbye, my dear. I trust you're having fun wherever you are, making new friends as I am here. I will see you in due course and we can share stories of our adventures. What fun that will be.

All my love, your Pussycat forever, Tony

XXXOOO

❧

We buried Lynn on November 26, 2022. Thirteen of us stood in a semicircle around the open grave. I read my letter to Lynn, then placed it in the ground beside her, and put her signature red hat on top of the urn. Then we each took turns tossing in a handful of earth, saying goodbye once more.

Epilogue

Tuesday, January 16, 2024
www.CaringBridge.org/LynnKotula

The day after Christmas we closed on the sale of Lynn's studio. Corde and I spent weeks emptying out the space. Several of the tables and many of the still life objects came home with us. Corde uses Lynn's favorite blue table as her writing desk, and Lynn's large black drawing table is in the bedroom, holding her Christmas cactus and several of her geraniums.

On the last day, I sat in a chair leafing through Lynn's catalog and breathing in the magic of that space, in which so much life, love, and creativity unfolded.

Then I said goodbye to it and locked the door behind me.

There is someone else living there now, an attorney named Randi. At the closing, I gave Randi a copy of Lynn's catalog, so she could see who had lived there before her and appreciate what Lynn did there. Her daughter sat beside her, paging through the catalog and becoming increasingly excited: "Mom, these are really good paintings!" Randi says they will invite me to a party once they've made the place their own.

The last day in the studio

After the closing I began working seriously on converting the CaringBridge posts into a book. I had made a couple of false starts after Lynn died, even printed out the entire journal, but quickly realized that it was too soon. I didn't have enough objectivity, couldn't make sensible choices about what to include, and how to shape it.

Last fall I looked at the posts again, but I didn't do any-thing—couldn't do anything—until the studio was sold. At that point I had taken care of all the tasks I had set out for myself: dealing with Lynn's estate; creating the catalog and memorial show; offering her paintings to friends and family members on a "pay what you wish" basis; making a comprehensive online archive of her work; and, finally, emptying and selling the studio. These were intensive, emotionally demanding projects. I guess I needed the last one out of the way before I could begin what I hope will be the most ambitious and fulfilling of them all: A book about our journey together, and what happened thereafter.

I started by stripping out the comments and editing the posts to remove repetition. I wanted to see how the story flowed if you read them one after the other. It came together quickly, and within a few weeks I had reached the last day of Lynn's life. I gave the book a working title of "I've got a lot to do" (from Lynn's last words) and planned to structure it in three sections: Living with Cancer, Dying, and Life Without Lynn.

The first two sections were complete, but there was something missing. So before tackling Life Without Lynn, I went back and restored some comments. This was transformative. These posts didn't exist in a vac-uum; they floated in a sea of supportive comments, encouragement, and insight from our friends. Once I included those, what had been a straightforward memoir became a dialog between Lynn and me and our friends. Those comments reveal where we got the strength to keep going.

They also changed the book in a more literal way because some of the best comments referred to material I had cut. This was like having an editor looking over my shoulder, saying, "No, kiddo, you can't cut that; it's important to your readers." I added back many of those paragraphs, and the book became more satisfying.

Most serendipitous of all, I found several places where Lynn had posted a response to someone. These are precious to me, as I want to include as much of her voice as possible. And then I came to one where she wrote: "Oh, Dear Life!! And how wonderful when we're able to win a bit or all of it back for a time." I knew immediately that this should be the epigraph. I get shivers every time I read it.

At about 10:30 one night, I reached the end of the Dying section. I felt exhilarated, wired, unable to go to bed. I was looking at the title of the next section on my screen, which I had originally called Living with Grief but then changed it to Life Without Lynn. This still didn't feel right, so I turned and asked Corde what she thought. She paused for a moment, then said, "Tony, I noticed today that you still wear Lynn's wedding ring. You're not living without her. You carry her in your heart." And with another shiver, I realized that "I Carry Your Heart" should be the title of the third section, and perhaps of the whole book.

A few weeks later I am in the kitchen, listening to music while emptying the dishwasher, when I realize that this is the radio station Lynn and I used to enjoy together, the one that caused me so much pain when I turned it on after she died. Now, instead of tears, I am smiling, thinking how much Lynn would enjoy seeing me like this, dancing in the kitchen, finding another happiness.

"We're so lucky," says Corde.

"Yes," I agree. "We are."

It's been more than three years since Lynn died. She is still very much with me, riding comfortably in my heart, and I find that I appreciate the richness of life, the gift of being alive, more than I ever did before we began our journey.

I don't know how this story will end. I guess I'll write another post when I find out.

For Lynn and Corde . . .

and everyone who helped us carry our tigers.

Acknowledgments

This is more than a book, it is the story of a life extended with the help of many people:

Dr. Matthew Hellmann and his nurses, Maureen and Sandi; Dr. Mark Bilsky and his nurse, Cynthia; Dr. Khalid Dar and his nurse, Arlene; Dr. George Krol and his nurse, Abby; and Dr. Jamie Chaft, Dr. Kenneth Weinstein, Dr. Alison Wiesenthal, Dr. Adrianna Kwan, and Dr. Sejal Morjaria. Each of these wonderful, caring doctors and nurses, as well as many other nurses, aides, technicians, and social workers along the way, was in part responsible for this book. If we hadn't had the good fortune to work with them, this story would have turned out differently.

Frank Marrocco helped me hang on to my sanity, and Sharon Messitte did the same for Lynn. My deepest thanks to both.

When I log into the CaringBridge control panel, I see that 186 people registered to read our posts. These friends—many of whom I didn't know, as they came from other parts of Lynn's life—provided invaluable support. The comments and emails that I quoted are just a fraction. There were hundreds more, each of which gave us strength, insight, and encouragement.

Most importantly, ten or fifteen CaringBridge readers explicitly encouraged me to keep writing after Lynn died. Without that encouragement, the last part of this book might not exist today or would be much shallower. Because of them, I explored my grief more fully than I would have thought possible, and many readers have told me that, for them, the third section, "I Carry your Heart," is the most valuable part of the book.

Nancy Hoffman provided the concept of "Carrying a Tiger," a lovely image and a perfect title. I've never met Nancy and only know her name because of the emails she exchanged with Lynn, but clearly, I owe her a big thank you.

Nancy Minckler posted the list of sixteen "cancer lessons" that beautifully reflect our own experience of living with cancer.

A man identified as "GSnow" originally posted, on Reddit, the piece about grief creating valuable scars.

When I thought the book was finished, I asked about twenty acquaintances to read it and let me know whether it was good enough to publish. In addition to a lot of encouragement, I received many useful criticisms and suggestions. It turned out the book wasn't as finished as I thought! Over the next few months, it became much richer, and to each of these readers I owe sincere thanks.

Paula Fitzgerald edited the manuscript, removing friction and adding innumerable small improvements, while David Wogahn and his team at Author Imprints designed the book and gave me a crash course in book marketing.

Finally, but certainly not least, Cordelia Pierson has impacted this book in more ways than I can count—and under unusually difficult circumstances. She encouraged me to write this story, then gave close reads and editorial suggestions to three different drafts. Can you imagine being my new girlfriend and having to read—no, volunteering to read—a story about my deep love for my late wife, again and again, while our relationship was still forming? No, I can't imagine that either, but that's exactly what she did. Repeatedly, Cordelia pushed me to go deeper—"What did this mean to you?" and "How did it make you feel?"—at great emotional cost to herself. The results are on the page, and Cordelia is still in my life.

About the Author

Tony Stewart has made award-winning films for colleges and universities ("A Union of People," "Skidmore: Concurrence of Ideas"), written software that received rave reviews in *The New York Times* and the New York *Daily News* ("Tony Stewart's Home Office"), designed a grants-management application that was used by three of the five largest charities in the world ("Riverside Grants"), and led the development of an international standard for the messages involved in buying and selling advertisements ("AdsML"). He lives in New York City with his cats, Boo and Lily, and with Corde when she is on the East Coast. *Carrying the Tiger* is his first published book.

For more information about *Carrying the Tiger* and to see more of the photos mentioned in the book, visit www.TonyStewartAuthor.com.

To learn more about Lynn and see her paintings, visit www.LynnKotula.com.

If you liked *Carrying the Tiger,* please leave a review at your favorite online bookseller so that other readers can discover it too. You don't need to say much; even a sentence or two is always appreciated.

Printed in Dunstable, United Kingdom

72018362R00184